I AM AN
ARTIST

ATTRIBUTIONS
INTERIOR TEXT FONT | Minion Pro
COVER DESIGN & TYPESETTING | Dennas Davis
EDITOR & INTERIOR DESIGN | Robbie W. Grayson III

SELF-HELP/Creativity | PSYCHOLOGY/Creative Ability
BODY, MIND & SPIRIT/Inspiration & Personal Growth

PUBLISHING INFORMATION
Traitmarker Media, LLC
www.traitmarkermedia.com
traitmarker@gmail.com
ISBN | 979-8-8690-1088-9

I AM AN ARTIST

(EVEN WHEN THEY SAID I WASN'T)

How To Restore Your Creative Identity

Dennas Davis

*This book is dedicated to my brother,
Doug, "The Painting Pastor," who discovered
he was indeed an artist.*

CONTENTS

Introduction | *vi*

-------PART 1 | TEARING DOWN-------

Chapter 1 | Who Is an Artist? | 17
Chapter 2 | Ball of Confusion | 31
Chapter 3 | Levels of Evaluation | 55
Chapter 4 | Talents & Magicians | 75
Chapter 5 | Creativity vs. Logic | 95
Chapter 6 | False Messages | 119
Chapter 7 | Seven Problems | 133
Chapter 8 | The Beastie Within | 169

-------PART 2 | BUILDING UP-------

Chapter 9 | The Blueprint | 183
Chapter 10 | Joy of the Journey | 211
Chapter 11 | The Lifeline | 225
Chapter 12 | The Personal Plan | 233
Chapter 13 | Healing Feels Good | 249

About the Author | *263*

Introduction

Have you often wondered about your creative side? Is there a version of you that you think just might be an artist, but you're not sure?

Do you already think of yourself as an artist, but you don't feel free to explore certain things? Or are the things you think, or have been told, only allowed for special, talented people?

Have you wondered if you're a "real" artist? If so, then this is your book.

You might even have been told flat-out that you *aren't* an artist. Many people have been told that. I have. Nevertheless, I am an artist.

I'm actually one of those people who grew up identifying as an artist from my earliest years. I was almost always considered the best artist in every group I was in, even in my art school.

I launched a design and illustration business the week after I graduated, and won numerous local and national awards. I have over five million books I've illustrated in print worldwide, with twenty-three titles. I have a gold record for my illustrations. Toys, clothing, shoes, and fabrics have been made from my work. I've done art for Forbes, Disney, Betty Crocker, Neiman Marcus, Time, Nabisco, and more. I've taught art internationally, and I founded my own art school in 2006.

By definition, I am clearly an artist.

Yet after decades of success, I was rejected as an artist. I was told by the people in charge of a new and very prestigious professional illustrators' organization that I couldn't join the group. They said I wasn't a "real" artist.

That really rocked my world. It took a while to come back from that foundational earthquake and to realize the deep insecurity even the most influential artists have. Elitism is just one symptom.

Since then, I've met and worked with thousands of artists, and one thing is clear: we all share the struggle of wondering if we're good enough.

I wrote this book for all the people I meet who don't believe they're artists but wish they were. I'm always working to change artists' ideas about what makes a person an artist. In this book, I hope to help you change your self-perception, too.

This book is about the artist in you.

There are so many reasons why artists don't believe in themselves. You're just like other artists if you've struggled with this.

As the owner of an art school for seventeen years, I've come across too many people with basic misconceptions about what makes anyone an artist, and there is a great need to clarify the issues surrounding artists.

It has taken me half a century of creating, selling, and teaching art, to learn enough to write this book. I hope you will believe what I have to say. I hope you can trust me, and I hope that you will be wonderfully encouraged as a result.

When I started this book, I wanted to have a specific end goal for you—a goal that goes way beyond just thinking one or two new thoughts. My goal is to get you to a point where you can be an active, confident, and happy artist.

Because you can.

I know this because I've seen it happen so many times I literally cannot count them all. It's become a familiar theme at my school. People come in who have never even held a brush in their hands. They leave knowing they're artists.

Children—who no one would say, "What an amazing talent they have"—come and take classes for years. You would never expect them to become professional artists. But because they love it, they practice. They improve. They realize their dream.

Everyone is creative in some way, and we know almost everyone enjoys art when very young. In my experience, a majority of people wish they could do art, and a whole lot of us really, really, love doing it.

Yet sadly, most people get the message that being an artist is only for a very few— for super-highly-gifted people—and that this is a group they're simply not a part of because they were not born that way.

This is completely false. You are a part of this group, especially if you're eagerly reading this. If your heart just jumped, then definitely, most definitely—you are an artist. Let yourself believe it.

I know it is true. I have seen every single person who began to believe it and made the effort, become accomplished. They all call themselves artists now. What stood in their way was their lack of belief.

I have been surprised so many times that I have finally stopped believing that art is only for an elite genetic group. Art is for anyone who wants to experience it.

You can believe it, too.

You're ready to go, too. No prior requirement exists. You don't have to sell something or win some award before you become an artist. Any kind of prerequisite goal or achievement is absurd. If you attain it, does that really mean you were not an artist before that affirming moment?

Of course not. That goal can be affirmed, but it's not what makes you *who you are.*

You are an artist.

So many obstacles prevent you from believing in yourself. For such an ambitious goal, we need a plan, one which we'll tackle together.

I wrote this book for all of us: the artists. You were born an artist, and I can prove it to you. Instead of providing long and complicated suggestions and solutions, I've divided this book into two sections to make it easier for you.

PART ONE (1) | TEARING DOWN

In the first part, I'll reveal the source of all these doubts, amplified by centuries of misconceptions. Then, we will dismantle the false blocks individually, setting you free to build a more authentic version of yourself.

Next, we will work together to more confidently rebuild your image as an artist. Understanding how your creative self can be repaired, improved, and maintained is essential so that you can move through your artistic journey with courage and joy.

When you get to the end of this book, you will find that I have another book coming out soon called *The Artist's Missing Manual—A Comprehensive Guide for How to Manage Yourself As an Artist*. In it, you will learn how to manage your artistic development to continue improving your artwork and move in your desired direction. You'll learn practical tools and methods that artists use every day, so that you can become the artist you've always wanted to be.

It's time to discover who you are. Momentum can be very important, and we have a little now, so please read Chapter 1 as soon as you can.

*Remember that the world
needs happy artists.*

Dennas Davis | *Franklin, Tennessee*

PART ONE (1)
Tearing Down

Chapter 1
Who is an Artist?

I'll never forget a crazy discussion we had in my freshman art history class. My professor asked us students to "define" art. We offered all kinds of opinions to establish limitations or to expand freedoms. Finally, someone got to the point: "Art is anything a human makes."

Then, of course, some smart aleck rebutted, "What about poop?" By the end of class, we couldn't agree on a definition.

People are often as poor at defining who an artist is as they are at explaining what art is. It has always surprised me when someone says, "Oh, no, not me. I'm not an artist—although I love art and like to draw and paint."

Here is a simple definition of art:

Art is people
sharing their viewpoints,
experiences, thoughts,
and emotions.

The artists pour themselves into their work, giving it out as a gift. They offer new ideas as well as old ones, shared beliefs as well as isolated ones.

Art is a dialogue among people—creator and audience and back again. Art is personal, and art is social. Art brings us together.

Most artists want to help people have a better life in some way, and offer their work as encouragement to others.

Some artists bring attention to the plight and suffering of particular groups of people, while others offer a respite from the world and concentrate on amplifying peace and joy.

Other artists want to make our environment more relaxing. Some artists like to do a little bit of everything.

Ultimately,
artists are those who
simply take the time and energy
to share their viewpoints with others.

One thing that stands out to me is a story many artists tell, usually as an adult or young adult. I've been a teacher for many years, and I've heard this story repeatedly. It's about the hurt and shame they experienced when they were young, and it goes something like this:

19

*My [adult mentor] told me
I was [deficient in some way]
and that I should [stop pursuing art].*

This story is full of irony because the adult who causes this damage thinks they're protecting the young artist now from experiencing this very thing that they will experience when they are older and likely more capable of processing it.

Imagine, for a minute, an adult telling a child never to play ball again because "You're probably not good enough to be a major league professional," or never to swim again "Because you should only swim if you're gifted enough to win a medal," or never to touch the guitar again "Because right now it seems like you're just not talented enough to be a rock-star."

That would be ridiculous.

Similarly, it's also absurd for anyone to tell you to stop doing art or that your art is not "good enough."

Good enough *for whom?*

But it's not only the mentor telling artists to quit: it's also traditions, societal norms, confusion, *and even other artists.*

In short, we all believe that true artists are always great, mysterious, and born that way. We believe that there are no varying levels of skills for artists other than the most excellent or complete failure. You're either an artist with a capital A, or you're not. It's a forced dichotomy of black/white or yes/no. Either you have it, or you don't.

This is not true.

Like art itself, we must add shade and color to this argument.

I want to show you how there's far more nuance than such a severe and limited duality. You were born an artist, but not because you were born with an exclusive talent that no one understands. *It's because you love it.*

But we are so afraid. Our fear sabotages our desire.

Imagine sitting in an art class where everyone is drawing a vase of flowers. You would never look at the person next to you and say, "Hey, you sure messed that up. You're not an artist. You can't draw! What are you even doing here?"

But artists say these exact kinds of things to themselves all the time. We are mean to ourselves.

The statement "I'm my worst critic" is very true in this respect.

Artists do not need any more discouragement. We are already hard on ourselves. All it takes is one tiny agreement that our doubts might be accurate to derail a young artist completely. That kind of discouragement often ends up in the abandonment of their creative process altogether.

So, back to my opening question, "Who is an artist?" Like many things, a short, simple answer comes to mind, but so does a long, more complicated one.

The simple answer is...

Everyone.

Do you like to share your experience? Do you like it when people share theirs with you? That's a scary question for some people, but we humans are a creative group.

I know that you believe, deep down, that you have a creative light inside you. This is true! In your core being, you want to make art. Zero reason exists not to pursue this dream. None at all!

In this book, we're talking about visual artists. I'm a visual artist. If you're reading this book, you have declared that you, too, want to be included in that group. Someone might have convinced you that you're not, but I assure you that you are.

Let's start with the four different kinds of artists.

The Satisfied Artist

The satisfied artist is a confident artist who works hard and encourages everyone interested to pursue art, too. They sometimes have doubts, too; but they understand that is a normal part of the creative process.

It has bothered me all my life
that I do not paint like everybody else.

Henri Matisse

The Injured Artist

The broken artist is the artist who has a hurtful story. They're damaged and often become stuck, not even able to create. Other forces and trauma have interfered with their artistic development.

Art is to console those
who are broken by life.

Vincent Van Gogh

The Pretender Artist

Even though they want to consider themselves
visual artists, the pretender artist has severe anxiety about the prestigious label "artist." Am I a real
artist, or am I just a copycat or a hack? Or, worst of
all, am I merely a "decorative" artist?

*The true work of art is
but a shadow of the divine perfection.*

Michelangelo

The Elite Artist

Finally, though successful, the elite artist seeks to dispel their doubts and bolster their image by elevating who they are. Dismissing all artists except a few popular ones (like themselves) creates the very doubt that plagues us all.

> *Art is the lie that enables us*
> *to realize the truth.*
>
> Pablo Picasso

Now that you know that you are an artist, which one are you? Let's figure it out. From here on out, it's just putting one foot in front of the other.

It's all downhill from here.

Chapter 2
Ball of Confusion

If we have such a hard time understanding the definition of art, how does a society determine if art is good or bad?

Most of the time, someone looks at a work and either likes it or doesn't. Some can appreciate art—even if they don't like it. But art that is compelling is visually attractive in some way that people agree on. This is *the visual* appeal of the work.

Visual appeal isn't entirely predictable, but many people like the same things. Beauty may be in the eye of the beholder, but only to a degree.

Many things are considered beautiful by almost everyone on the planet: sunsets, gardens, butterflies, and rainbows. So, some general consensus exists.

We usually know *exactly* what things we like and what things we don't. When it comes to visual art, though, we often have less confidence. I may like something designated as "bad" art and be repulsed by something defined as "good."

Who makes these designations?
Who agrees on what good art is or is not?
Why is art so weird sometimes?

It's essential to distinguish the idea of quality in art from its monetary value. Quality is just one of many things that add value to art. Let's look at how that works.

People who study and curate art for museums, websites, magazines, books, auctions, and galleries have a more significant say about the value of art because they're the "facilitators" of how art is and becomes valued. These experts assign value to art based on many factors.

Popularity and visual appeal are essential, but other significant factors affect the value. These other factors are often problematic because only the elite know or understand them. Sometimes, almost no one agrees about the value of a work, yet critical experts still assign a "good" designation.

Modern art can be the most confusing. We can see a work we do not like and then find out that it's worth several hundred million dollars. Art is glorified online, yet we often scratch our heads at how amateurish or unattractive it seems.

We read about strange "artworks" that are entirely conceptual and make no sense to us. We see works in a museum that seem so ludicrous that we laugh out loud.

Modern art (1860s-1970s) has glorified experimentation for the last 150 years. You will find much more agreement about what is good and see a more comprehensive appreciation when you move to older and more predictable works of art. The Avantgarde movement has done the most to change and challenge us but also to confuse us.

You may have read about *the cans*. In 1961, an artist sealed his own excrement— yes, poop—in 91 steel cans, just like food is sometimes packaged. The cans were mishandled in the 1990s, which resulted in an expensive lawsuit.

One can had begun to leak. The lawsuit awarded $35,000 simply because this art is considered to be valuable—not the poop, but what the artist did with the poop. You may question the value assigned to this work, but it is art, and that's very confusing to most people.

Millions of dollars of canned poop
is just weird.

I've seen some curious modern artwork in museums: four old vacuum cleaners in a plexiglass box, lit by an overhead office-style fluorescent light; off-the-shelf boxing gloves simply hanging on the wall; a carefully crafted sprinkle-donut in the bottom of a paper bag that looks delicious but isn't really edible. All of these works are by some of the most influential artists of our day like Jeffrey Koons and Robert Gober.

One story I like is how someone once accidentally dropped their gloves in a museum. Everyone carefully walked around them, discussing what the artist was trying to communicate by having gloves on the floor.

*It's not an urban myth—
it's really true.*

This illustrates just how bewildering art can be to us. Something is wrong when we can't distinguish between a common accident and purposeful modern art.

One artist, Banksy, has made fun of this confusion by placing his parodies of art in museums. He secretly stuck his own work to the walls when no one was looking.

The value of something is determined by how much one will sell it for and by how much one will pay for it. If someone is willing to exchange money for art, then a value has been created by a seller and a buyer. Back to *the cans*—some of these cans have sold or auctioned for well over $100,000 each, with a single can fetching $275,000 in 2016.

You would think visual appeal and popularity would be what makes art more valuable, which is sometimes true. However, basic market forces and other factors influence the price of artwork significantly, often eclipsing the value of its visual appeal.

Sometimes, the thing that affects art the most in the high-end art world is importance. Knowledgeable people say which art they think is most important based on a set of self-selected criteria. Then, the item attains a new value separate from the visual appeal.

Art auctions bring in millions for the most scarce of these most valuable works. The auctions themselves push values even higher. Imagine the competition over cans of poop. Apply that to less repulsive works.

Sometimes, these separate values are obvious. Say that you found a horrible painting in your attic. It's a portrait of a mother and child, but the colors are garish, and the hands are poorly drawn and distorted. Perhaps, the child's face looks like something from a horror movie poster. But then you read the signature, and it says, "Vincent."

You are now a millionaire because you found a Van Gogh painting in your attic. The quality of the portrait doesn't matter because it was painted by Vincent van Gogh. You could find a used handkerchief that Mr. Van Gogh borrowed from someone, and it would have value because Vincent blew his important nose into it.

We all agree this is an essential yet ugly painting of a mother and child. Why? Because most everyone also agrees that many of Van Gogh's paintings are some of the most beautiful ever created. This agreement comes from the visual appeal of most of Van Gogh's paintings.

The value of this painting would be *much higher still* if the painting was of a sunflower or even one of Van Gogh's better baby portraits. The point is that there is a value entirely separate from the value of the painting itself. It is a value of agreements—how much we value Van Gogh's other paintings, the fact that we like those visually appealing paintings, and their importance to us.

Also, the tragic story of his life and the fact that he is long gone and can't make more paintings enormously affect the value of his entire work.

Since we agree on the importance of his best artwork, Vincent's finite supply of paintings is just one more factor which increases its value. It's just essential supply and demand.

Almost any famous person can pick up a few art supplies, paint a canvas, and sell their painting more easily than less well-known artists who have honed their talent for decades. Their popularity in other arenas affects the value of their artwork.

Factors That Affect the Value of Art

VISUAL APPEAL—Most people like its appearance because it follows composition standards such as balance, emphasis, appealing content, etc.

Popularity—Ideas can take hold and propel a work based on current trends, or a famous personality can add importance to a work through association.

Supply—There is always a limited number of works by one artist.

Competition—Sometimes, the need to win elevates the price of an artist's work when it is auctioned off.

Historic Relevance—When a significant meaning existed at a time in the past, sometimes these meanings lose their relevance.

Surprise—Originality gets harder and harder to find. Something new can surpass appeal simply because it's different.

SHOCK—Being rude also has a certain kind of value. It gets our attention.

ART MOVEMENTS—These happen in the high-end art world but are not typically within most people's experience.

CONTENT—Art can make statements that are separate from visual appeal, which can be socially, financially, or politically motivated, seeking to influence in a particular way.

PURPOSE—Sometimes, an artist makes their work unappealing on purpose or presents it in ways that go against societal norms. Graffiti is one example of this.

NETWORKING—Who you know and who knows you always makes a significant difference in how your work is exposed and marketed.

Exposure—Art that more people view becomes more powerful and often more valuable.

For a moment, consider the various factors that can increase the value of artwork. All except the first can elevate the value of a work of art, regardless of its quality. Often, these external, agreement-based values are only decided by a select group of people, as in my example of the Van Gogh portrait.

A few select art critics and dealers can elevate artists and their work for reasons that may confuse many viewers. Conversely, you have works of art with a low visual appeal and a separate elevated value that many people need help understanding. When many of the most valued works of art are confusing, then all artwork becomes harder to evaluate.

Sometimes, extreme elevations of artwork occur, and we read about dramatic sales in news stories. A small group of important people will compete to pay vast sums of money for a small number of artworks.

Valid reasons may exist for the excessive values assigned to works of art by these elite few—but should be shared if most people are excluded from that process and need help understanding it.

A small group of people agreeing on the importance of a work of art isn't a bad thing. Money is one of many ways people agree on the importance of a work of art.

*It is my dream to create an art filled with balance,
purity, and calmness, freed from a subject matter
that is disconcerting or too attention-seeking. In
my paintings, I wish to create a spiritual remedy,
similar to a comfortable armchair that provides rest
from physical expectation for the spiritually working, the businessman, and the artist.*

HENRI MATISSE

What is most important is that art has the capacity to make the world a better place. It can be a small thing for a limited number of people or a widely known movement that affects almost everyone.

Art that elevates people's experience can be in your aunt's living room or on the side of an urban building. It can be in museums, galleries, offices, schools, and homes.

Art is often at its most powerful when it's private and highly personal, such as a card a child makes for their favorite teacher.

When art is larger and in a public space, it has the ability to affect more people. It is easy to believe that public art is more important because it is more visible and accessible.

That may be true when the art's purpose is to affect society, but if the artist wants only to offer an exhilarating moment of beauty, then who is to say that more people seeing it makes the art itself of a higher quality? The placement itself makes it more powerful, not that the art is better than other works.

It's not easy to find and purchase great original art. Most people don't have the budget for it. While not a great system, money is how we assign value to art using dollar signs, so only people with a lot of money can enjoy it.

There are solutions, though.

Museums bridge the gap between some of the highest quality artwork and everyday people who could never afford it. This makes important artwork accessible and adds even more value by affecting the most people.

It is okay if a group of people values a work of art in spite of their not being knowledgeable art collectors or dealers. If a piece is relevant to them, if it's enjoyable to look at, if it's appreciated—then it is as valuable to those people as artwork that costs far more money.

Your uncle's portrait of the family dog can seem more valuable to your family than a Picasso, just because it is so much more accessible and meaningful to you.

If any number of people agree that they appreciate a work of art, then that work has shared value. Simply because a group of people agree on value, it exists. Whether those people are as small as two or as large as the whole of society, the agreement is significant. The art is just as crucial to each individual in either group, whether large or small.

If you like your work, and your parents do, too, then that is a shared value. If your friends like your work, you should be happy about that. These people are the most important in your life, and they are assigning value to your work.

Don't waste your energy comparing your work to what is in a museum, a fancy gallery, or an auction. That is a different kind of importance, which comes from different values and different people that you don't even know.

If you took the time and effort to share your viewpoint and put yourself into a work of art, and someone appreciates it—wow! That is a fantastic thing. You must be an artist!

If you want that to happen, but it hasn't yet, don't say to yourself, "Then I must not be an artist." Instead, if you are willing to take the time and make the effort, say to yourself, "I'm not there yet. But I'm going to be."

Remember this—
the value of artwork
can be extremely confusing.

Visual appeal is important and a variety of factors tends to impact and elevate the value of the most famous artworks. The visual appeal of artwork also has *levels* of quality, which makes evaluating art even more complex.

If you rated paintings on a scale, with ten as the best, every artist would have a range of numbers they would hit. There are always some of the best artworks in every artist's body of work, from artist to artist.

Appeal, however, is different.

One artist may have worked for years and have some unique gifts. Another might be new and have to work harder to achieve their goals. A whole spectrum of visual appeal exists. We will explore this spectrum more in the next chapter, but all art has validity on its level of appeal, whether done by an amateur or a professional.

One More Thing

One more thing that needs to be clarified about the value of artwork is reproduction. We look at prints and small screen depictions of large works of art all the time. These miniature versions are removed from the original several times, going from canvas to photograph, to print, or to a screen.

Sometimes, a work is sculptural or environmental, filling an interior or exterior space in an installation.

A reproduction will never be able to convey the actual power of its original. The bigger or more three-dimensional it is, the more difficult it is to convey. Pigments used in paint differ significantly from the pixels and printing inks we use in reproductions.

Size also matters more than you would think. Imagine comparing a house you've only seen in photos on your phone, to one you have physically walked through. You might get an idea of the nature of the house, but you want to see it for yourself.

The best works of art are impossible to describe easily, even in photographs. They have to be experienced. But we often only view the most famous artworks in small photo reproductions and base our evaluations on them. If the work is impressive in real life yet bland or ugly in a photo, we need clarification about what makes art good.

So, art that has been highly elevated to a level of great importance will have many different factors that affect why it is so esteemed. While we want to believe that visual appeal is the only thing that elevates art, it is seldom true when looking at the most expensive and renowned work. This is the main reason people need clarification about the quality and value of art. It is hard to believe that these other things can make a difference, but they do.

As a society, we need clarification about the nature of art. We all need help understanding why art is designated as good or bad. Don't let societal confusion about art intimidate you and hold you back from pursuing your own art.

#1

Chapter 3
Levels of Evaluation

My wife makes incredible dinners because she loves to cook. I help by opening a bottle of wine sometimes. She makes such good food that we have difficulty finding restaurants that make a meal more unique than what we eat at home.

When I'm alone, though, sometimes I just make a cheese sandwich and grab a beer. After these different kinds of meals, I'm no longer hungry. While I enjoy a simple cheese sandwich, it is not on the same level as one of my wife's meals.

With art, you are often expected to be the chef at a 3-star Michelin restaurant, making a 9-course dinner every night, or everyone should go hungry. Sandwiches would be unacceptable.

We know this isn't true. We know that there are levels in the quality of art, just as there are levels of quality in everything, but the idea persists anyway. Then, it becomes a weird requirement when a young person wants to pursue art. "No, no, no… you are not supposed to attempt art if we can see (or even suspect that) you will not be one of the very best."

So, you can't make food if you are not going to be able to cook in the best restaurants in the world. Many people have been told that you cannot train as an artist if you only want to "cook" for your friends and family. It would be a "waste of money and time." Gah! I hate these kinds of thoughts.

It's time to let go of that misconception and be happy wherever your art takes you. If you need encouragement, ponder that during Vincent Van Gogh's nine years as a painter, he created nearly a thousand paintings and 1100 drawings.

He sold only one painting. His paintings were only understood and appreciated by three people, two of whom were his brother and his brother's wife. Everyone else didn't think he was a "real" artist. Other artists, critics, and regular townsfolk thought he was wasting his time.

Art is highly subjective. "Beauty is in the eye of the beholder," we are told. And we are also often told precisely which things are beautiful and which are not. The people of Vincent's day were told that his work was terrible because it did not look like "good" work of his time.

There is pressure on artists to perform at a certain level and often to do so without even being trained. Add to that the many factors that need to be clarified about what makes art valuable, and artists get stressed about doing any art.

*So, how do we evaluate and
appreciate all levels of art?*

There is so much more than black and white. We need to learn to accept more levels of art than the two extreme endpoints. There is much to discover and enjoy between "worthless" and "priceless."

Composition and visual appeal are complicated subjects. Artwork involves many elements: accuracy, self-expression, style, technique, color, balance, contrast, and more. Each aspect can affect the overall composition. That means many things are increasing the visual appeal—or decreasing it.

This creates a vast spectrum of quality and appeal, with myriad values between the worst and the best compositions.

Expectations

Most people enjoy art that falls into the category of, "pretty good," as opposed to "the best of the best." In real life, the opinions of the experts don't influence our likes and dislikes nearly as much as those experts think. When it comes to others' artwork, we accept so much more. We love to see kids make art. We encourage our friends to make art.

If a famous art critic came to your house, would you consider hiding some of your favorite things? Would you hide any artwork you have done yourself? Or devise an excuse for why you like it that has nothing to do with the art? Would you say something like, "This is a sentimental piece!"

All the confusing expectations surrounding visual art are even more intimidating when we apply those expectations to ourselves. We might even feel like the things we enjoy creating are not real art. We have the most difficulty believing "I'm an artist."

Expectations can make us think we're cheating when we like things that aren't recognized as great art. It gets worse when we think about making our own art. Then, we are so afraid of high expectations that we don't even begin. We can't take the risk. We have been convinced that only the top level is genuinely valid.

Unrelated Personal Bias

Personal likes and dislikes also affect this spectrum of levels. Everyone who evaluates a work of art has their history and quirks that inform their judgment. Imagine entering an art contest and you don't win because your painting reminded one of the judges of a bad experience they had as a child. Or, what if the other judge hates a particular shade of orange that you used? Evaluations are affected by personality, too.

I once entered my clay sculpture artworks into the county fair. I was in the eight-to-twelve-year-old group, and was around ten years old at the time. I was really excited, because I had made a special display board for the twenty small sculptures I had made of cartoon characters. Some were my own characters, but many were famous cartoons that everyone knew. Everyone who had seen these said they were very good, and I wanted to win the art competition for my age group.

When I arrived at the fair, the judging had all been done and I had not won anything. I was surprised to find that my sculptures had been reassigned to a different category than art. They had been moved to the collector's section, which was for baseball cards and stamps. Worse, the first place in art had been awarded to a boy who had made some designs in ball-point pen on paper, using a toy called a spirograph. The toy did all the work except for choosing colors.

I was quite upset by all this, but it was over. Nothing could be done. My dad tried to fix my mood the next day by giving me an "Honorable Mention" ribbon that he had acquired and said that the judges had decided later to give to me. It didn't help.

I felt like I had been told I was not an artist and my work was not valuable. I lost to someone doing work that anyone who bought the toy could easily produce with little effort and no experience. None of this was true, but that is how I felt. That's what the art judges communicated to me.

I understood quickly that the toy art fooled the art judges. They lacked knowledge of what was happening, which was an illegitimate valuation of the winner.

But more important was what I didn't realize until much later—that the judges had mistaken my clay pieces for things I had purchased, things that had been so well made that they believed them to be manufactured for hobbyists to buy and add to their collections.

In reality, I blew the judges away, so much so that they didn't even believe a person my age could create such works. Their bias and lack of understanding could have derailed me, but thankfully, they did not.

Deeper Appreciation Levels

Knowledge is another factor in art appreciation. The more you know, the more you see, and the more you appreciate.

Years ago, before we had children, my wife and I had a chance to go to Europe and spend time with dear friends. We traveled through the Burgundy region of France, and I made a new friend, Ellis. One day, Ellis and I were shopping for wine in Baune. Baune has some of the finest wine cellars in the world, so we were trying not to get in over our heads. But we did anyway.

We went into a lovely place, and they took us down into the cellars—the caves (pronounced "kahves"). The floor was gravel, the walls were stone, and the ceilings were arched, flowing right into the walls. Rows and rows of giant wooden wine barrels lined the sides, with a path down the middle.

Our guide took a small wooden mallet and tapped off the large stopper on the top of a barrel, explaining that this was their best red wine.

Then he lowered a two-foot-long glass tube with a bulb on the end into the hole. He squeezed up some wine and then put some into the glasses he had provided us. Ellis and I looked at each other with eyebrows raised.

I was new to this. Ellis had explained that when you taste wine, you're supposed to sip and slurp, getting air into your mouth with the wine to get the full flavor. Then, you pour what's left onto the floor and move on to taste another wine.

We looked down at what was in our hands: their best wine. We sniffed deeply, which was terrific; then, we tasted it. I remember being shocked at the flavor. It was so excellent. It was overwhelming. I hadn't known anything could taste like that and did not even know how to react or what to say.

Ellis had a wide-eyed expression, too. He looked at me, and after a moment, he said, "This wine is bigger than we are!" And I said, "Yes! It is." And then we tossed the rest to the gravel floor with a flourish. I was pretty happy when I purchased three bottles of their "smaller" wines.

When we drink good wine, we appreciate it. When we can taste a truly great wine, we can have an entirely elevated experience. You suddenly realize that good wine is only good, not great, and you now have something far better. It does not mean that you never drink good wine, though.

Sometimes, merely exemplary or mediocre wine is OK. We cook with it and drink the rest. Often, *decent* is the highest level we need.

Some people know wine well; to them, the finest wines are all they can enjoy. They have the means and the knowledge from their experience to drink only the great stuff.

There's nothing wrong with that. However, if they start thinking that only great wine is worth anyone's attention, which makes others feel bad about liking and drinking only moderately good wine, that is different. They have become elite and look down on anyone who cannot be like them.

Sometimes, art elitists make us feel bad about our painting, even when we're just trying to learn how. Ignoring these folks and surrounding yourself with artists who appreciate all levels is best—good artists, who are confident enough to encourage others.

My friend, Jim, is a poet and musician. When he goes to a concert, he has a different experience than I do, analyzing and appreciating much more than the "surface of the music." He knows a lot and listens to technique and quality aspects I can't even hear, much less appreciate.

We both love music. He is glad that I enjoy it on my level and that sometimes I enjoy music he can't. His more profound knowledge of it causes him to hear flaws that don't get through to me. It's okay for me to be me and for Jim to be Jim. We've had breakfast weekly for over 30 years, and we talk about music and art a lot because we both enjoy learning more about it and comparing our creativity.

My wife and I both love to watch home improvement shows. We enjoy many shows together, but she watches one type of show that I can only watch for a short time. DIY disaster shows make me crazy!

Learning on my own, I have fixed many things over the years. If a show has a guy telling his wife he can fix something and then makes terrible decisions, often ruining parts of their home, I just can't watch without becoming upset. My knowledge and understanding get in the way of the entertainment. I leave the room, head to my studio to paint, and let her watch. It works out fine.

But what I don't do is tell her she shouldn't appreciate or watch that kind of show simply because I know a little bit more about plumbing and carpentry than your average person. She doesn't make me feel bad about my cheese sandwiches, either.

So don't worry about other people's standards for art. Don't apply an art critic's knowledge and appreciation to your artwork, especially when trying to figure things out. Just do your work, and keep learning to improve at your own pace. It takes time.

Art progression is not a linear thing. Great artists don't always produce great work. Think about that baby painting by Vincent.

This means you will do different kinds of work: good art, bad art, and probably a fair amount of in-between work—all the time. All artists do. The most valued artists suddenly find that even their bad work is valuable, and it confuses everyone, even them.

*Every artist will create
two kinds of artwork.*

I propose a different kind of evaluation that applies to all artworks.

LEARNERS—artwork that is valuable as a learning experience, and

KEEPERS—artwork that is valuable both as a learning experience and as something to be proud of, show off, or share with others.

You always start off creating many more Learners. As you progress, you make fewer Learners and more Keepers. Eventually, most artists will be creating mostly Keepers if they stay at it long enough.

If artists stop creating Learners, their work stops progressing as long as they repeat what they already know.

Some people disdain that, too. They say the artist has stagnated and is no longer growing. But if that makes the artist happy, and they have a happy audience that appreciates that work, then what is there to criticize? Only that they are not doing it "the way I would do it," which is not a valid reason for negative criticism.

You can use Bob Ross as a great example. His work and videos make the world a better place and many people happy. You won't find his paintings in museums or collections, but I'm glad he painted them. They're essential in many ways.

When you think of a famous artist, think about all the Learners they made, attempts that missed the mark that may have never been seen. No one publishes them. They're usually not saved by someone other than the artist, or they go into the trash bin.

That means every well-known artist you could compare to has held part of their work back. What you see is an edited version with all their blemishes removed. All their Learners were eradicated. We always expect people to put their best into their portfolios, but it is not a realistic portrait of who they are as artists.

Don't be fooled into thinking "real" artists always create work on the level they show to the public.

CHAPTER 4
Talent & Magicians

This chapter is important. Come back and reread it after you finish the rest of the book. Really, please do this. I'm not joking. It's not very long. Read it as many times as you need to.

"I don't know if she has any talent, but she loves painting,"... "I don't think my son has real talent but loves drawing,"... and "I don't have artistic talent, but I always draw and paint. I love it."

What is this magical thing we refer to as talent? I hear statements like the ones above all the time. We are convinced we'll probably not do well at art, even if we enjoy it.

But what if someone doesn't have this magical thing called talent? How can they ever hope to accomplish anything?

Harry Potter is all about elitism. Only those born with a special gift can be wizards. The author even makes it hereditary, bringing in an element of racism. Everyone else is a Muggle and always will be, no matter what they do. You are either a wizard, or you never will be one.

I enjoy the movies! Don't get upset at my critique of Harry Potter. I just don't like how this underlying assumption reinforces the idea of elitism and that talent is some kind of a magical birthright. No one wants to be called a Muggle. It sounds terrible, even dirty. We are secretly afraid that we are artistic Muggles, wanting to fly but only ever being able to sweep the floors.

In the real world, science tells us that certain traits and gifts are hereditary. More and more, as we keep investigating and learning, we find that experience is what matters the most, though.

Experience and learning are the majority of what we call talent. Hereditary traits are rudimentary, and just a few things are passed down from parent to child. One of these things is what attracts you, what you love to do. That is so very important.

Develop Your Talent

Where are baby Michaelangelo's paintings? Baby Monet's? Baby Norman Rockwell's? We don't see their work from an early age because they had to develop their talent. They worked for years, making "learners" and creating better and better work by practicing.

But what about raw talent?
These three artists had something that
most people don't. They had
something special to build upon.

You're right. These guys are up at the top regarding extraordinary super-power gifts. Just like Simone Biles, Sting, Michael Phelps, Adele, and many others we see at the top of their fields.

But you do know they all worked hard to get to the top. And here's another thought that I think is significant: Why do we not see creative dynasties? When an artist is stellar, we rarely see subsequent generations of the family reach the same heights—not close, even.

Back in Freshman art class, I remember being told by one of my instructors that "the world is filled with extremely talented people who don't do anything with it, and because they don't develop their talents, they won't ever reach their potential." The professor meant that some people can draw accurately more easily than others.

This is a narrow view of talent, so I no longer feel his statement is accurate. But what is truer is that they have been damaged and turned away from art, or they didn't inherit a love for making art, which is the most important thing.

Talent is simply a mixture of a few simple genetic traits combined with a ton of focus, love for something, and extreme determination. You've heard the phrase, "10 percent inspiration and 90 percent perspiration." Well, there is a lot of truth to it. You can also say, "10 percent genetic traits and 90 percent what you do with them."

Everyone has genetic traits and gifts. Within that 10 percent, only a tiny portion of super-gifted characteristics exist. That means you have most of what anyone else has to work with. Super-gifted people who love what their gifts can do can take what they have and make the most of it. They can rise above others and achieve great things, which is rare.

- *Most swimmers are not gold medalists.*
- *Most writers are not Nobel prize winners.*
- *Most artists don't have their works in museums*
- *Most singers are not included in the top 10 charts.*

Not many people are born with a perfect swimmer's body, like Michael Phelps. But almost anyone can learn to swim, and many slow swimmers enjoy swimming. I sure do; everyone moves faster than I do in the water.

You don't hear anyone say, "Don't ever swim again unless you have that one-in-a-million swimmer's body that will take you to Olympic gold." That sounds ridiculous.

The truth is that everyone has a set of traits to start with. You can think of it like a plot of land to develop—raw land that is yours to develop.

Some people might get a stream, and others do not. Some people create structures to catch rainwater and get as much water as a stream. They can often accomplish as much or even far more than someone who takes their streams for granted.

You work with what you have. No matter how rich it is, developing your land takes a lot of work. But what is the most important thing about your raw land? What is that thing that makes someone get the most out of their plot? Is it the soil, the rain, the stream, the climate, the flora, or the fauna?

To get away from the analogy and back to artistic capability, what is an artist's most important set of traits? Is it their visual analysis, creativity (inventiveness), tendencies, spatial understanding, patience (or lack of patience), or fearlessness?

All of these play a role, but there is one thing that is far more important than all of them. It is your desire. I love making art. It makes me happy and fulfilled no matter what happens after I've made it. When I was young, I loved reading craft books and art magazines. I have always enjoyed making stuff.

We Love to Create Art

I remember long ago hearing that love was the most misused word of all. But no other word seems to fit when we're talking about passion for something. We are passionate about art and creativity. That is the main thing. Above all, passion for doing art is the most important thing for artists to succeed.

And when I say succeed, I mean make art that makes you feel satisfied and that you enjoy sharing with others—no more than that.

If your other traits align with your desires, that makes everything easier and can sometimes propel certain people to stardom. It's not stardom that makes someone an artist, though. Any more than a number one hit makes someone a musician or a gold medal that turns someone into a gymnast.

I have so many stories that have surprised me and made me question what I had learned. The most important one is from my art school's first year in business. It's the most important because it was the first time I was challenged in my preconceptions of what makes an artist.

In my first class, I had a mom sign up her teenage daughter for summer art lessons. The mom had some drawing experience. She sat in the back of the room and drew some lovely sketches, but the daughter was new to art. She didn't draw or paint well at all. I even wondered why she wanted to try art. Thankfully, I kept that thought to myself.

As I taught the daughter, I just looked for the good things in her work and pointed these out. I was encouraging, but not unrealistically so. I tried not to lie about what I said was good, such as, "That's great!" when looking at work that wasn't great.

Instead, I looked for something good, like a shape that was more accurate than the others. I pointed this out and explained how accurate it was and how she could use that skill again.

I remember believing that "the mom is an artist, but the daughter is not." I never expected her to go far with her art or be as good as her mom. Wow, I could not have been more wrong. She improved slightly that summer, but they did not sign her up for the school year. I figured that was that. But I later learned they didn't have enough money.

So, they show up again the following summer, but this time is different. The daughter could draw! She had style, accuracy, and technique like her mother—and even better. I was astonished. We talked about how she had improved so much, and I wondered how she managed to find some kind of mega art course for the year.

She and her mother beamed back at me and said last summer made the difference, that my encouragement had lit the fire of her creativity. She worked all school year independently, doing what I had told her to do and more. She developed her talent, which did not even show in her work at first.

That year, this same girl applied to Savannah College of Art and Design and won a full-ride scholarship!

I realized that my assumptions were all wrong. People whom most art teachers would easily dismiss could learn to be great artists. I set out to keep up with the encouraging teaching style for sure!

Since then, I have seen this story replayed over and over. We've taught several thousand students now. I have been amazed by them!

For years, one student, Olivia, never really showed what you would call raw talent. At first, she didn't stand out. But she loved art. And I mean, *really* loved art. She worked on her art all the time. She began in one of my classes at age six and continued with our art classes every year until she graduated high school.

Her work suddenly improved in a pattern I've finally come to expect. One day, as I looked at it with a new appreciation, I thought, "I didn't remember it being so good."

Olivia also went to SCAD on scholarship after being in my classes. Her work had become so amazing when she left us that the school president plucked her first project at SCAD off the wall when he walked past a student display. He held it up and said, "Let's use this on our next brochure."

This is the president of a premier art school, noticing a student's work that stood out—in a sea of some of the most talented students in the country. Yet she was so ordinary as a young art student that I don't remember her work until she got to high school.

Then, almost overnight, her work became some of the best I'd ever seen. She developed her skills and learned how to become "talented." Olivia now works designing the art and graphics for Universal Studios theme parks!

Many of my students have struggled at first and later improved. A new student will begin taking classes, someone who might have been discouraged by many art teachers after seeing their initial work. Yet, they will stick with it because they enjoy art, and we don't discourage them. We show them how to draw, and after a while, they're doing fantastic work!

Sometimes, it's several years, but it happens. It's so fun to see this transformation. It usually occurs suddenly. In just a few short weeks, their work improves by leaps and bounds in

What is the one thing that all these students have? That one special ingredient? It's not talent. It is a passion for art. All these students' parents said, "They love art!" They kept doing it, over and over, enjoying the process.

You love art! That is it. That is all you need to build upon. Add as many exclamation marks as required right here.

The most important thing for everyone else to do is to stay out of the way. During these early stages, young artists are often told some version of, "You need to find something else to do. You're no artist."

This is devastating to them. The one thing they love and want to do is taken away. Children believe what they're told. It only takes one person making one statement to negatively influence a potential artist.

I know this because I've heard that same story from a hundred adults. One person stepped in and ruined their love of art. It was an awful and, sadly, self-defining moment for them. But there is hope for people who have a story like this.

Almost every artist struggles on some level, fearing that they're not good enough, not a real artist.

The most important thing for the artist to do is to get help. Undoing that moment, if it occurred, takes time and determination. Counseling is awesome. Don't ever be afraid to get help.

I tell people who are scared of counseling that it isn't about finding out what's broken inside of you so that you can fix it. No, it's about discovering that the thing that feels so broken is just fine. We just were told it was broken.

You are okay.
You are not broken.
You were born an artist.

I know this deep in my soul. While I wrote this chapter, it was hard to see because I cried as I recalled all these fantastic stories. The good stories make me weep for joy, and the bad stories make me mourn.

So there is one more important thing for the artist to do. That is to be patient. You have to stick with it and be patient with yourself. This is why I'm almost finished with a second companion book on how to develop your art.

Art is like learning a language. It's harder for some than others, but everyone needs much time and practice to become proficient. If you love art, take the time to develop your talent. Don't apply expectations of any kind.

Just enjoy yourself.

Artist Abilities Comes From A Variety Of Sources

1. Talent
2. Gifts (Heredity)
3. Visual Analysis and Visual Disconnection
4. Spatial Perception/Flat Mapping
5. Visual Memory/Forgetfulness
6. Inventiveness/Consistency
7. Fearlessness/Timidity
8. Patience/Impatience
9. Preferences (What Do I Enjoy Doing?)
10. Ambition
11. Experience
12. Training Insights (Making Things Easier)
13. Training Techniques (Best Methods)
14. Experimentation (Discovering New Things)
15. Practice (Repetition)
16. Personal Tendencies (Personal Patterns)

Chapter 5
Creative vs. Logic

Historically, much research has been done into how creativity works in human minds. At some point, the scientists decided that our creative mind was isolated in the right side of our heads and that the left side was just for logical functioning.

This led to speculation that people were divided into two primary groups: "right-brained" or "left-brained" people. Those accountants and lawyers were left-brained, and the artists were right-brained.

This led me to speculate that very few people have empty sides of their heads on the right, so we must all be fairly creative.

I used to tell people who talked about not having a "creative bone in my body" that *that* couldn't be true, or they would be walking around leaning to the left because of all the space on the right side of their skull. It's a funny picture, but it makes you think. If everyone has both sides of their brain, what makes some seem more creative?

More recently, researchers have been saying that it's not quite so hemispherical and that both sides of the brain are involved in most operations. Such killjoys. We like the whole side-to-side thing, and most people still stick with that paradigm no matter the truth.

But when this was a new theory, Betty Edwards wrote a book, Drawing On The Right Side Of The Brain. It is a revolutionary book; you should read it. Edwards helps us understand why we have trouble seeing the world the way it looks and why we tend to draw things badly.

We draw things the way we expect them to be—even when it's not what we see right before us. The book has some great exercises to help artists discover how to draw more accurately.

In this chapter, I want to explain one of the main reasons we tend to draw unrealistically:

logic versus creativity

Before we begin, I want to clarify something essential: drawing cannot be right or wrong. Artists always draw what they need to be drawing. Drawing is essential and very good for you, even if you hate the results. Drawing can, however, be accurate or inaccurate.

When you don't like a drawing you've made, it's not because you drew it inaccurately. It's because you didn't draw it the way you wanted to. The fact is that we usually want to draw accurately. We want to make our drawings look like how we see the world. We strive for realism, but it's tough to do.

That means we usually don't like our drawings. While making things look accurate is challenging, that is exactly what we desperately want to do!

I have seen very successful artists specializing in realism repeatedly make the same inaccurate shapes. When trying to be realistic, even some old masters got it "wrong."

What is it that causes us to draw things poorly? In a word, logic. And the logical part of our mind is not just one half. It is incredibly dominant. Logic is in charge—all the time.

Even when an artist understands the influence of the logical mind and fights against it, drawing accurately can take significant effort. The analytical and practical part of our mind is necessarily strong, always taking over in order to keep us safe. We must use our understanding of it to navigate and stay safe.

Is that dodgeball flying right at my face? I know it is because it's getting bigger and bigger, very fast, which means it must be moving closer and at high velocity, too. It's time to duck so my nose isn't smashed.

We don't think that slowly, but our logical, practical mind does all that thinking in a split second. We react so quickly that we don't even seem to think at all. It's truly remarkable. We see the ground and instantly know whether it is flat or tilted. We know that when we approach a staircase, we should change our cadence.

We see things on a table, and we understand them logically. The table is perfectly flat and horizontal so that nothing will slide off. The cylindrical glass has a flat bottom and sits flat on the table.

We see the opening, and because we understand our angled viewpoint, we instantly know it's a circular opening without thinking. All these things are automatic. We don't think about knowing the logic of our world; instead, we experience it.

Let's apply that logic to our drawing, though. The top of the table is a rectangle. This is accurate and true. So, draw a rectangle first. The floor is flat, and the legs are all the same length. Draw a flat line for the floor. Draw a leg from each corner of the rectangular table down to the floor line.

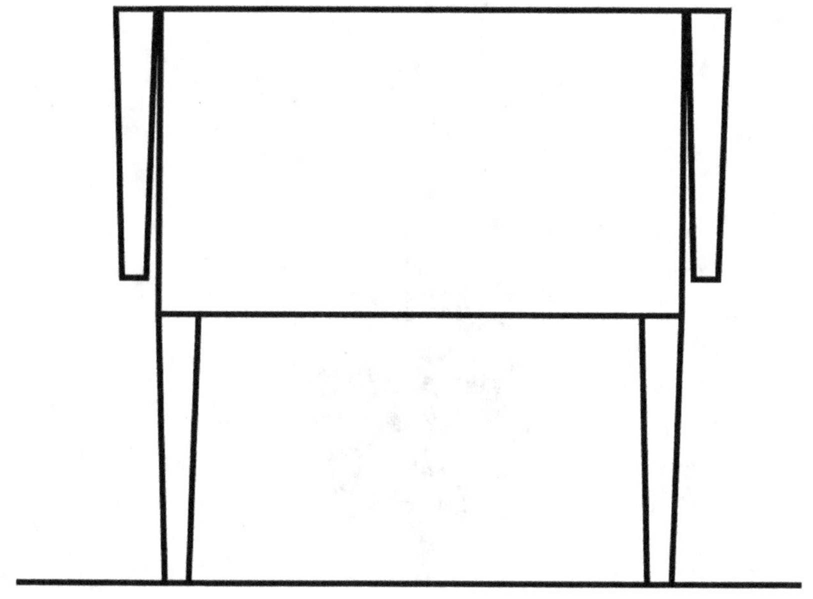

(It's impossible to do this)

But look at the glass in this photo. If you want to learn to draw more accurately, you must trust me for a moment and stop reading. Get a pencil, paper, and eraser. Just do it. Go now! A book has endless patience to wait for you to come back.

Welcome back. Thanks for doing this exercise. If you just pretend to do it in your head, it won't work. But if you take a moment and draw this without looking ahead, you will learn something amazing.

Draw this photo about twice the size that it is in the book. You can blend and make shadows or draw some lines to depict it. Don't worry about it. There is no test, and no one will see it except you. Just do your best to draw it accurately, twice this size. Then, come back and continue reading.

Draw now.
Come back only after
you have finished.

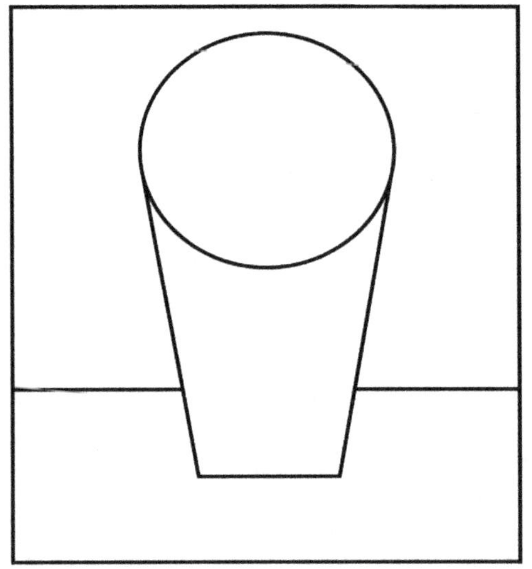

An artist drawing only logically would draw the two straight sides, a circle on the top and a flat bottom sitting on the flat table. We know this is true, but it looks wrong because it is so inaccurate. What we see does not look like what we know.

*What we know will be different
from what we see.*

When we draw a map, we mark an area's logical truth. When we paint a landscape, we reproduce one viewpoint of that area. The landscape has more than one view, though. What does it look like from the other side, on that hill in the distance? Well, it is entirely different.

The landscape will look different even from 5 feet away to the right. It will look very different ten feet to the left or standing on a balcony two stories up.

Every single room, every single still life, every single animal, person, or landscape—has thousands of viewpoints. Logic only tells us a diagram or map of things. Only our eyes can allow us to understand each unique view—and only when we don't let logic fool us.

When logic is in charge—remember, to keep us safe—it makes it super-difficult to counteract. It takes more practice than you imagine to remove the influence of logic on our drawings.

Now, let's look at the glass you drew. Don't worry if you're not entirely happy with it. I'm writing this book to help you not worry and figure out how your creative side can work for you. If you drew a very accurate glass, you already know this part and would agree with the following instructions. But most of my readers will feel there is room for improvement.

Some people will draw something almost identical to the logical drawing the first time. That's your starting point. Everyone will draw somewhere in-between logic and realism before being trained. My point is that logic is on one end of the spectrum, and accuracy is on the other, and we're influenced by both. We have to find a compromise between what we know, and what we can see. It's difficult to figure out because our brain needs both viewpoints to be satisfied only as we're drawing. When we view it afterwards, our brains instantly recognize when a drawing does not match what we see. The logic isn't even remembered. It's invisible to us that we were trying to satisfy logic, and now we can only wonder why our drawing doesn't quite look realistic.

Our brains always tell us to compromise between views as we draw–the logical truth of the object vs. what our eyes tell us.

Artists routinely draw what they see with compromise-induced logical inaccuracies. They will draw an ellipse on the top of the glass, but because they know it's a circle, they will draw a bigger, more circular ellipse than they see. Then, looking at the bottom of the glass, they will only see the front edge of the bottom, which is, of course, logically flat, resting on a logically flat table.

The eye sees a curve, and the mind knows it is flat. The artist then draws a much more flattened curve than they see. It is a compromised curve and a compromised circle/ellipse.

And it is challenging to believe either one or the other entirely. You would never believe the logical drawing above. But I'm telling you that you also don't believe what your eyes see.

You didn't draw the bottom as curvy as it needs to be. You drew the top way more circular than it looks. If you had a real glass on a real table, the logic would be stronger since it would be in all three dimensions right there in front of you. The logic is more evident, and you would draw it even less accurately.

Here is the thing about ellipses: they are flatter the closer they get to your eye level when moving up or down. They are more circular the farther away from your eye level, moving up or down.

Again, if you want to learn how to see and, hence, how to draw more accurately, get a plate or saucer right now. Anything circular will do, paper, plastic, or ceramic.

Welcome back. So, sit at a table or counter and close one eye. Hold the saucer about six inches above the surface. This is a circle but also an ellipse from your viewpoint. Now, very slowly, raise the saucer until it reaches eye level.

It becomes all flat, straight lines, and you're looking at the edge. There is not a visible ellipse at precisely the height of your eyes.

Now, keeping one eye closed, very slowly, lower the saucer to the surface, watching to see how it gets more circular and less like a flattened ellipse. Repeat this a couple of times. Watch closely.

This means that the line at the bottom of the glass is way more curved than at the top. That is what you are seeing with your eyes. But what we know in our logical mind makes us compromise so much that we do the opposite. The top is drawn more circular than we see, and the bottom is drawn more flat.

Typical Drawing

We always tend to draw the tops more circularly simply because we see that it's an entire circle. The logical mind says, "You know that is a circle." So we push it into too much of a circular shape, a compromise.

Then, we draw the bottom more flattened because of two things that make us compromise.

*1. We know the table and the bottom
of the glass are flat, too.*

*2. We don't see the bottom as a full circle. We only think
of it as a line connecting the two sides. Our mind says,
"You know that is a line going from one side to the
other on a flat table." We see the curve.
The only thing we can do is compromise.*

Here is a set of drawings to help you see what I'm talking about more clearly.

Accurate

Difference

The accurate drawing looks "right" to our brains, because it conforms to the visual view. The typical drawing I showed was closer than most students get, but you can see how far off it is by seeing it added on the right in lighter-colored lines.

How can I walk you through a simple drawing and know how it will turn out? I have never met you. I'm not super-natural. I didn't trick you into doing it a certain way. What's my secret?

The secret is that every artist always does it that way. You were born a typical artist.

If you drew the glass accurately, you have already trained yourself to counteract basic logic. You learned to see through to the viewpoint on your own at an early age. You moved yourself away from what everyone usually does and became exceptional. This is what is generally referred to as talent.

Still, it is just the result of an intense desire to draw accurately, combined with an excellent analytical ability and a lot of trial and error that you likely don't even remember anymore. Now, you're good at seeing things as they are without outside help. That's fantastic! And exceptionally rare.

Every artist needs training and practice to see accurately. A rare few can self-train, but most of us need to read a book or two and take some suitable classes with an understanding and encouraging teacher.

The training is not about how to do something better, like swimming better at the pool, but rather how not to do something that holds you back. Learn not to let the logic push you into making compromises. Remember, a camera has no logical brain and always gets things perfectly accurate from its current viewpoint. If you can just get that brain out of your way and learn to look differently, you can draw more accurately.

It's more of a zen thing to leave the logic and live in the viewpoint while you draw. Just know that it is not a quick fix. Practicing will improve your work, but it takes some time. The logic is strong in you.

Chapter 6
False Messages

Artists hear a lot of messages. Many come from decades and even centuries of entrenched misconceptions. They trickle into our media, even confusing mentors, and can further confuse and discourage artists.

Let's look at a quick rundown of things you probably believe without even realizing they are false messages. You can stop letting them hold you back by identifying and understanding them.

1 | The best art comes from angst & suffering.

This idea has taken root, especially in the late 20th and early 21st centuries. Maybe everyone is so stressed that angst is an emotion we deal with more often. I don't know, but I do know that artists can work from a place of joy and peace just as easily as from a platform of anger and outrage.

In music, we listen to protest songs, blues, visions for the future, love stories, mindless dance tunes, and more. No one maintains that one style of artistic expression is the only valid one.

No style of expression should be disqualified for visual artists.

*Art washes away from the soul
the dust of everyday life.*

PABLO PICASSO

*Art is unquestionably one of the purest and
highest elements in human happiness. It trains
the mind through the eye and the eye through
the mind. As the sun colors flowers,
so does art color life.*

JOHN LUBBOCK

2 | FAMOUS ARTISTS ARE THE BEST ARTISTS.

Surprisingly, this has only sometimes been true and even a rarity in the last 60 years. A well-known artist may be excellent, but some are mediocre, doing things others could have done just as well or even better. Some famous artists got lucky, may have just tried something outrageous for the first time, or have known certain people and were included in the elite high art scene by association. That's good for them! This is how the world generally works. Recognition is rare, and there needs to be more of it to go around.

Of course, this is only a problem when you allow yourself to believe your art needs to be better simply because you are not getting recognition from a wider audience.

3 | ARTISTS CAN'T MAKE A LIVING.

Poor Vincent. He never had a career or income. His story and others have created the vague yet persistent idea that artists can't make a living. There are two huge problems with this myth.

People do lots of things that they don't make a living at. This supports the idea that you should only create art if you can be a professional artist.

Play ball. Swim laps. Sing songs. Write stories. Make Art. Enjoy life.

The other reality this crazy idea ignores is that the arts are a significant part of our economy. Many jobs are primarily for artists, and being an artist benefits every other profession, either directly by adding skills or indirectly by promoting positivity and releasing stress.

4 | Real artists don't have to practice.

All artists always practice. Professional artists practice a lot to get to where they are, and they have to continue to practice as they continue to create. Practicing is the fuel that keeps the train moving down the tracks.

5 | Instruction kills creativity.

Nope, that's not true. Instruction allows artists to do what they want without as much frustration. This bad idea comes from the glorification of self-taught artists and from teachers who don't know what to do.

It takes a lot of work to teach yourself. Most of the time, it doesn't work. Think about teaching yourself to speak another language without any help. You might be able to do it with a two-language dictionary and no one to talk to, but it would be so complex that most would quit. Also, it would take far, far longer to accomplish anything when you teach yourself.

While it's an amazing thing to see a self-taught artist, and they should be applauded, it's not the norm or required, and training does not "ruin" an inherent inner muse.

6 | REAL ARTISTS NEVER HAVE TO LOOK AT WHAT THEY DRAW.

Haha! This is crazy! I have no idea why anyone would think this. Every artist looks at references to draw realistically. If an artist can draw something without looking, it is almost always because they have memorized how to draw that thing by looking at it and drawing it many times.

A few artists can draw from a deep understanding of what the world is like in 3D. They learned this early by drawing from life, having some gifts in spatial and visual analysis, and a strong drive to artistically capture the world accurately.

Along with the love of doing art, these things helped the artist learn how things look in a way that eludes most people. They can pull up 3D models in their mind's eye and use them to draw.

7 | Accuracy is the right way.

When an artist says, "I drew it all wrong," they mean they drew it inaccurately. I often hear this in classes: "I didn't get it right!" This comes from a desire to draw accurately. In these cases, right means "I want accuracy," and wrong means "It's not what I wanted."

Striving for accuracy is a great goal that artists should work towards. Accuracy allows us to depict the world the way we see it, like the glass of water on the table. Conversely, drawing inaccurately could be more comfortable for us.

Some artists strive for accuracy; when it's not easy, they leave it behind and work only in the abstract. Some artists misunderstand the need for practice and training, listening to all the false messages and, sadly, believing they cannot improve.

Anyone can learn accuracy if they want to. You learned to write with a pencil, so control isn't a problem. Seeing is the problem with accuracy. The last chapter addresses the root cause of humans' poor vision—logic. In my second book, *The Artists Missing Manual,* I will have several exercises to help you draw more accurately.

Perfect accuracy is not the end goal for many artists. It's the beginning. When you think about the art you love the most, does it follow accuracy completely? Or is there an element of expression from the artist that is not what you would see in a photograph?

Monet was so expressive. Matisse and Picasso left accuracy behind. The impressionists added color and expression to their accurate drawings.

A camera is perfectly accurate. If you want accuracy, become a photographer or a photographic realist. All other art removes itself from the real in some way.

Most of the work of expressionist artists results from a strong understanding of accuracy and a willingness to depart from it.

There are also loose techniques that look fantastic and need accuracy, but people don't often realize it. Impressionistic art must have a highly accurate drawing underneath. Impressionists have a more challenging time being accurate because they must do so with fewer strokes and less surface manipulation. They must be more accurate than anyone else, or the loose strokes will look awkward instead of beautiful.

For instance, a figure in the distance with a single brush stroke for the face must have a face-shaped brush stroke. You have a monster in the distance if the stroke is a horizontal blob.

Even abstract art benefits when the artist can draw accurately. We enjoy the abstract for many reasons, but relevance and similarities to the real world are two of them.

Our classes use accurate and inaccurate instead of right or wrong. This helps us realize what we're trying to accomplish and understand why we don't like the work. "Wrong" doesn't give us any direction for improvement.

CHAPTER 7
Seven Problems

This chapter points out a whole slew of problems about learning art. The good news is that once you know the problems, you can fix them. Each problem will be presented along with its solution.

Before we get into it, I want to explore how art problems are perceived because this can significantly affect how well the solution will work.

Here's a little story.

One day, a young couple comes home from their vacation to find a leak in the bathroom. It's not a huge leak, but water is all over the floor and dripped into the room below. The floorboards and a chair are soaked. The house is cold.

The couple sit down and cry. Their house is broken! They loved this house. It was going to be the place to raise their family. Now it is all gone because it broke.

They sigh heavily and sadly leave the home, shutting the door forever to look for a new house.

What a dumb story I just told you. It was thankfully relatively short because I couldn't spend much time on it without feeling badly about writing more. It simply makes no sense.

Here's my point, though. The idea that the house is broken is a gross generality. Generalities are seldom helpful when evaluating something complex, such as a house.

If the electricity went off, you wouldn't declare a house broken. If the roof were getting old and leaking, you wouldn't give up on the entire house. These are specific problems that need specific repairs.

The story should go like the following...

The couple calls an HVAC company that also does plumbing, and they get everything fixed in a couple of hours. They remove the water and purchase a new chair. The heater just needed a new wire where a mouse had chewed it. The faucet in the bathroom needed a new rubber gasket. Everything is as good as new. Then they enjoy a nice meal and admire their lovely new chair.

So, it's still a boring story, but at least it's a happy and realistic ending. I, for one, feel much better now.

Another complex thing is you. You are a bit like a house. In your psyche, you possess what we will call a foundation, a basement, and an attic. There are systems like electricity and plumbing. You are, of course, even more complex than a house.

When you want to learn something as big a subject as art, this adds complexity upon complexity, which is way more complex than a simple house.

The house is an excellent analogy for thinking about creativity and artists. When people look at a drawing they've made and see that it's inaccurate, they naturally feel badly about their effort. But then all of the false messages kick in, and the self-talk becomes, "I guess I just wasn't born with enough talent."

This is the point at which many artists stop trying. They close the door, thinking the house is broken, when they just need some drawing lessons.

However, artists are also unlike a house because creativity is much more mysterious. This makes it even harder to figure things out and presents the first of seven major problems.

1. The Unknown Problem

Artists look at themselves and see something they don't like or think is broken. They think, "I cannot seem to draw things right." They cannot identify the unknown problem because they don't have enough knowledge to understand this specific concern, and they don't know what to do. Most people don't even know that creativity and drawing skills are fixable.

When the mind doesn't know specifics, it defaults to huge generalizations, lumping everything together.

The resulting conclusion is, "I'm not an artist." The whole house is broken. So many artists mourn this enormous loss and shut the door, leaving the creative house forever, all because of one or two specific issues which can be fixed.

The whole dang house is broken.

Here is the thing, though. The fact that you are able to see a problem is essential for being the artist you want to be. Think about it. If you look at your work and see nothing to improve, you are not able to evaluate its quality. You would be stuck drawing poorly and never know it. Understanding that you need to improve is an essential skill that artists always deal with. It's part of being an artist.

Solution

Don't generalize. Do not abandon art because of one specific goal you don't know how to accomplish. Every single thing you want to do is learnable. If you can see you need to learn it, then you have the most essential skill you need.

Remind yourself that all artists struggle and that everything can be learned. Talent is developed over time, not magically acquired.

2. The Delayed Response Problem

You might ask, "But what about when I didn't realize my work was bad?" Well, this is also a normal part of being an artist.

Every artist has had a honeymoon experience with their art. You finish something, and you love it. You're very proud, hardly believing you could produce such awesomeness.

A week later, it's like a different work. You see all the flaws you were blind to only a week ago. With this new viewpoint, you now hate it—and yourself for being fooled. You thought you had a winner, but it was just another loser. This kind of emotional chaos can make things worse than if you had never tried. So, many do stop trying.

None of these assessments are true, though. What happened is that a part of the work is excellent, and that stands out. You are naturally excited and proud of this great part, especially if it's a breakthrough for you. You are so happy that you don't notice any other things at work. It becomes such a bright light that everything else is temporarily overtaken by the brilliance.

You did something good.
That's what you want to do.

There are no such things as failures in art. You always learn from working. You always learn from doing. Your whole goal as an artist is to create, learn, and grow. It's a journey, and exploration is the biggest part of it. You cannot waste your time attempting to create any kind of artwork. You will either create one of two outcomes: Learners or Keepers. Every artist creates both.

The reality is not that you were fooled or that the work is bad. The truth is that the work, like most artwork, is a combination of strong and weak parts. There are excellent things about the work and some challenging areas. The excellent things we've been working so hard for are there, which can blow our minds. We are blinded, temporarily, to any problems. Later, we can see things more clearly after the glow of accomplishment has subsided.

It's only the fact that noticing the problem areas was delayed that surprises us and makes us think we're dumb about our own work. Then we do the same thing but in the opposite direction! We swing over and focus only on the weaknesses, which now eclipse the good parts just as much as they originally made it hard to see the bad parts.

We need a balanced view.

That moment when you finally see the parts that need work is vitally important. That's when you can see more objectively. This critical moment allows you to evaluate your work and processes and make necessary corrections!

How could any artist function otherwise? Either fix this work, redo it, or carry the learning to the next work. Or all three.

Artists have to remind themselves to stay balanced and not to swing from one extreme to the opposite. Fear pushes us to expect that we are not good enough, and that very fear tends to create an extreme backswing.

Solution

Be more aware of that moment when you see things you dislike in your work. Instead of generalizing this work as good or bad, let yourself see your artwork as a collection of both Learner and Keeper parts. Try to remember that the good things are still very good.

What you do when you see problems in your own work is entirely up to you. It will either move you forward, as all normal growth processes should, or it will be misinterpreted and cause you despair. Don't believe all the negative messages. Take the learning and move forward with it, even if the objective perceptions were delayed by a honeymoon period.

3. The Knowledge Wall Problem

Moving forward and learning art may be a new idea to you, and how to begin is probably not something you've thought about. What is the next step to take? If you don't know, you're at a standstill. You become stuck simply because you don't know what to do next.

The problem of not knowing how to move forward is exacerbated by the mysteries of art, human creativity, and psychology. If you don't see how everything works, you can't fix anything. The knowledge to proceed seems to be behind an impenetrable wall.

Most people assume things can't be fixed at all. The only reason we know house systems are fixable is that there are experts we've heard about our whole lives who make a living fixing them.

Plumbers, electricians, roofers, painters, etc., all know how to fix these systems. They learned about the components, practiced, and became experts. A house is not surrounded by a cloud of mystery like the creative mind.

So while house systems and the corresponding experts dedicated to fixing them are known, the systems themselves and their components are still quite mysterious to most people. Fixing a plug that doesn't work or figuring out why the washing machine won't drain is behind that wall of understanding. Not only do we need to know the specifics, but we also need to know either who to call for help or where to learn how to fix something ourselves.

Solution

When discouraged, write down the things in your work(s) that may be causing this feeling. These may include poor accuracy; which part of the work is causing the discouragement, whether or not the composition is boring, etc.

Use the blueprint at the end of Chapter 9 to figure out the specific area(s) that could be the problem.

You must learn to experiment and not be afraid to do so. That is how you gain knowledge! Find help for fixing the problem AND experiment with specific changes to see what works best for you. The second book, with the lessons on how to fix things, will help a lot. Also, you can look on YouTube, search engines, books, and friends. You can do this.

4. The "Standards" Problem

What makes you *you* is a complex group of complex systems. It is hard to understand. We don't even know the systems for our creativity, much less anything about those systems. But there arc no experts to call. There is no colorician or techniquologist who can turn some bolts and insert skills into us.

So we look to a class and a teacher to learn, but art is a gigantic subject. A drawing class can help with drawing because the teacher knows about it. A watercolor class can help with watercolor, but where do watercolor and drawing overlap? Don't you need to draw before water coloring? (Yes!) What about using thick acrylic paint? Can I paint loose enough so that I don't need to know how to draw accurately? (This is a common misconception, and you need to be more accurate with loose painting techniques rather than less).

Art teachers are not always trained in the art of teaching. Freelance teachers are sometimes not even trained in the art of art. If they do have a degree in art, there is no guarantee that they have been taught well or comprehensively because every art school is different.

There is no consensus in the world of art regarding what is essential training for either art teachers or artists themselves. Every program stands on its own. Every teacher decides what to teach and how to teach it. There is no standard curriculum or even an agreed-upon outline for it. There are only some basic ideas that have been repeated for a while.

One of the most telling ways to demonstrate how unregulated art concepts are is to do an internet search for the "principles of design." I did this today and found a site explaining "The 4 Principles of Design." Another site had a chart showing "The 9 Principles." Another one had "The 13 Principles."

The most common number used for the principles of design is seven, but not all seven principles are the same—you can find many variations. I found one site that had The Seven Principles of Design, but two of them were the same: harmony and unity, each with almost identical definitions.

Many things taught in art schools are not all that important to artists once they get out in the field. Other important things are not covered well or at all. Some things that have been taught for years make it harder to make great art.

Electricians are certified. Doctors and lawyers have to pass extensive exams. Even realtors have to pass tests and know their standards. But there are no true standards when it comes to art.

In an art school, you'll usually find one teacher doing watercolor classes and a different teacher doing
figure drawing. The drawing teacher may not know
how to do watercolor well, so they can't teach it.

This means the instruction is compartmentalized,
even if you're at a great art school. I have seldom
seen someone who graduates from art school with a
full understanding of all the systems of art and how
they work together.

Out in the freelance teacher realm, it's more difficult.
You will likely learn only to emulate that one teacher's style because that's what they know well. They
may not know very much outside of that thing they
always do. They may not even know how to teach
you to do their one thing, just telling you to follow
along, hoping you'll somehow pick it up.

So, finding a good class is not guaranteed, and finding a teacher who knows various techniques, media, and styles is almost impossible.

SOLUTION

Finish reading this book. It includes many practical references, including a great set of principles that will help you design better.

No one will have all the answers in one place, but you can learn to manage your own learning and take control of your vision for your art.

Don't get stuck by following one teacher's odd rule or obscure statement.

5. The Copying Problem

I don't play golf well, but I play way better with my brother, who plays a lot. He tells me exactly what to do during the game, and I follow his directions. Afterward, when he's not around, I have no idea what to do because he hasn't taught me how to figure things out on my own. My score goes right back to what it usually is.

I know artists who have taken lessons and made good-looking paintings in class. They copy the teacher and the teacher's painting. But afterward, they don't see how they did it and can't create their own paintings at the same skill level. It's very frustrating.

My mother took classes like this for a while from a very nice teacher. She loved the work she had done, painting snow-clad barns and landscapes. After we moved, she struggled to paint these subjects for years and gave up several times.

Then one day she saw her own painting in a garage sale. It seemed like someone had stolen it right off her wall! But it wasn't hers; another student of that same teacher had done it. It was almost identical to her own painting.

She went home extremely distraught after this, believing she had been a fraud. She could only copy paintings like all the other students did. She didn't paint for years and never enjoyed it as much as before.

I wish I knew then what I know now. She could have learned to paint anything she wanted! She just needed to know how to find and control the specific problems within the systems of art. All she had learned was to follow each step of her instructor as he painted.

He never revealed true knowledge, such as how colors interact when mixed. He just gave a recipe for each color as they went along. In his classes, you only learned the colors for one painting at a time. But you didn't learn why, or how, the pigments worked together.

Because it was simply copying another person's work, there was no composition or drawing instruction, which are essential skills that must be learned and developed.

SOLUTION

If you've experienced this, start today with a new plan for moving past the misconception that you can't learn what the instructor learned. You will be more prepared going forward, as you begin to take control of your own artistic development, finding ways to expand your knowledge and skill set.

6. The Plan Problem

Art students are usually left on their own to figure out what classes to take, and they must put together their own plan for their art education. It's a crap shoot. Most beginners don't know what they like to do, nor what their tendencies are. Often an artist's strengths usually lie in areas different from the art they like the most.

This is why a lot of people who want to learn art never get around to it. They don't know how to get started. Many end up buying a book and starting there (which I think is an excellent idea, of course). But which book do you buy first? Color theory or acrylics? Oil landscapes or pencil portrait drawing? What brushes do you need? What kinds of paints? Should you start with watercolor, acrylic, gauche, water-soluble oils, open acrylics, fluid acrylics, or standard oils? Which brands? Which pigments?

Sometimes people take a course that sounds great, such as "How to Watercolor European Villages." However, if you've never been taught how to draw accurately, or anything about perspective, no amount of amazing watercolor technique will make your work look satisfying to you.

People take classes in this way and are immediately embarrassed. They often quit, because they say to themselves, "I couldn't even do a beginner class in a basic technique."

The big idea of "Learning Art" as a general subject is daunting. It's like being told to build your own house. However, only learning one specific technique without understanding how things fit together isn't the way to solve this problem. The unrelated parts need to have context. Even if you know how to install wiring, pour concrete, and hang drywall, if you don't know where and how those parts fit together, you still can't build a functioning house.

The good news is that building your foundation and establishing a personal edifice of art are absolutely doable. It's not going to be quick or magical, but it's completely understandable. It's not as daunting as building a house by yourself. It's more like learning a language, and you can do it if you keep at it.

You will need help with this. You need to have specifics, as well as an understanding of all the systems that each specific issue is contained within, and also how all the systems relate to each other as a comprehensive whole.

A standard plan of action with clear instructions for how everything fits together will help you refine and manage a personal art education plan for yourself. Everyone finds it is so much easier to get started when there is a plan with a set of instructions for how to proceed.

Imagine building a house and starting with the kitchen appliances. They are the most exciting place to begin if you like to cook, but they won't work sitting out in the middle of your plot of land without water and electricity. You need to build the kitchen for the appliances to go into. Before you can do that, a kitchen needs utilities, a roof, walls, and floors, and, most importantly, to be on a stable foundation.

Here's a scenario I see a lot that can cause beginners to think poorly of themselves simply due to lack of information. Artists who have not had good instructions, and used cheap brushes with poor quality paint, will make a judgment about paint being too hard. They often never want to paint again, generalizing that, "paint is not for me." They shut the door to one side of the house and proclaim themselves an artist who only does drawings.

In my art school, we take a comprehensive approach, helping every student understand the basics before they figure out what they want to do with their art. When I realized more people needed help understanding art and making their own plans, I decided to write this book. A book seemed like a great way to reach creative and artistic people—people like you.

This all might sound intimidating to you, but it is simply a set of parts that fit together. Having good instructions for building your plan will help you know what to do, every step of the way. It's like a blueprint for building a house.

SOLUTION

Start your planning now, by doing only one thing at a time. Keep putting one foot in front of the other.

You learned multiplication tables. You can learn this too. Art is not simple, but it's doable, and this book is going to help you do it.

7. The Context Problem

If you don't know anything about systems and context, everything can be scary and confusing, even if you have a library full of how-to books. After you have a blueprint that puts everything in its place, you can figure out almost anything.

People who have never lived in a modern home with electricity, running water, heat, air, and so on, they may have trouble knowing where to get help when something goes awry. If the refrigerator stops producing ice in the door, people may have no concept of where the water comes from, how it turns into ice, wires, motors, plugs, faucets, or anything.

Let's say a home repair library exists where it is possible to learn how to fix everything in the house. However, no context exists for any of the books. It would be difficult to know which book is the right one for the problem. They pick up a how-to book on fixing a water heater and then a book on insulating an attic.

Nothing in these books helps with an ice maker. On and on it goes, with the wrong solutions. They are overwhelmed just trying to find the right book. They need an outline with categories and an index for every book in the library.

Then they can find the right instructions and discover a few simple steps is all they need. They order and install a new water filter in the fridge and, like magic, the ice maker works again. Only it's not magic. It is knowledge combined with context.

Figuring out your house of art is daunting because there are so many overlapping components. Context is key.

Say someone wants some help with how to draw an animal. They don't like their first drawing because the stripes they drew don't look accurate. They don't look like they are on the animal. It looks like they drew a flat cutout and then pasted a pattern on it.

The artist wants to know how to make it look more realistic, so they go to the library and find a book on visualizing in 3D. The book is all about perspective. It explains dimensions, horizon lines, and vanishing points. It's terribly confusing and poorly written. It has no animals in it at all, so it doesn't help.

Then they find a book on how to draw animals which seems more promising. It is full of skeletons and muscles and how to make fur look fluffy. The artist becomes ever more frustrated.

Most art books are super specific, as are most art classes, focusing on how to draw one thing or how to paint one kind of technique in one medium. The beginning artist has to navigate a sea of possibilities when knowing little to nothing about how the possibilities fit together.

A class on drawing may or may not have time for individual instruction. It's difficult to commit to an 8-week drawing course and only draw fruit in bowls, or guitars and puppies, never getting any help for the stripes on a zebra.

What this artist needs is a foundational lesson on how to make stripes wrap around a dimensional form. The lesson might utilize a cylinder with stripes, or striped cloth, but the concept will apply directly to zebra stripes on a zebra body. In fact, a lesson like this will apply widely to all sorts of patterns on all sorts of objects.

SOLUTION

A blueprint for your house of art, with a library of art systems that are categorized for context, would be great for knowing how to get started, and for maintaining your growth as an artist. This blueprint is in Chapter 9.

These seven problems I've described are creativity killers. It's no wonder so many people who want to learn art, never actually do.

As we continue, I want to show you how to learn art and how to make learning art easier.

If you know what to look for and where to find it, you can continue your training as an artist with confidence. *The Artist's Missing Manual* (coming soon), is a companion manual I've written for artists, which will help get you going.

This is a book in which I share practical things like methods for organizing references, finding creative inspiration, the seven stages of making art, color basics, and much more. You'll take your own journey from there. You can do it!"

Chapter 8
The Beastie Within

The part of the house that affects everything else the most is the foundation, which also encloses the basement. When a foundation is great, no one notices. It's invisible, covered up by shrubs and flowers. A straight and level house means the foundation is doing its job.

Likewise, the basement is not a living part of the home. You don't bring your guests down to see the old furniture and furnace lurking in those shadows. These are the hidden places, which, nevertheless, are essential to the home.

Your subconscious mind is powerful and hidden too. Jim Watterson, the creator of the Calvin and Hobbes comic strip, did a great job making Calvin's subconscious mind actually look like a horrible basement, with flooding pools and junk floating around.

His dreams would be managed by a "staff" of little Calvins, digging around, looking for old films down there. The little Calvins played the films and couldn't believe how crazy and scary they were, wondering where they came from. It was a funny way to imagine how our subconscious dredges up fanciful dreams when we're asleep.

While helpful, analogies never quite fit perfectly, so I'm going to switch to a different one because we need to think in terms of mobility. You're on a journey, moving through time, navigating your creative endeavors (as well as everything else in life).

I like to imagine my subconscious as a giant lumbering beast that is powerful, yet plodding, not very open to new ideas, and not able to analyze or predict what is about to happen.

Even though it isn't the part of the mind that thinks things through and makes decisions, the subconscious affects those decisions profoundly. This beast can be downright mean to you, if you let it.

The subconscious, or lower mind, trusts one person more than any other, and that is the conscious mind. That is you. Anything you've ever told it is true because it doesn't know that you lie or exaggerate things. It doesn't understand that you don't want to stay there whenever you put yourself down.

The lower mind takes everything literally.

If you've ever said to yourself, "I'm not a 'real' artist," then that has been heard loud and clear. It is now the gospel truth. If you've told yourself you won't ever be able to do something, then you have made it so much harder to ever do that one thing.

If you say to yourself, "You dummy!" every time you make a simple and normal mistake, but don't routinely call other people dummies, then your subconscious believes that you, as a person, are dumber than others.

So you are riding this big beastie through life, yet you don't have any reins to control it. You can cry and kick and whack the top of its head, but it stubbornly lurches in dark directions you don't want it to, simply because you have trained it to believe that is where you want to go.

You can't suddenly change "its" mind, by telling it not to go in a direction that you've said is the right direction for years. If you've fed yourself a lot of negative thoughts, one or two positive ones won't be enough for change.

You have to retrain your subconscious. You must use positive talk, instead of negative talk, when referring to yourself and your abilities. All. The. Time.

The good news is that it doesn't take too long to see real change. Start thinking good thoughts about yourself and your whole mind will respond. It does take practice, and it does take purpose. Reminders and positive notes, or little signs, are good, even if they seem silly to you. You need to be kind to yourself and retrain yourself to believe that you can do art.

Because you can do art. I know this because there is no way on earth you would have read this far if making art wasn't a profound desire in you. That very passion is your true talent.

Another amazing thing is how the subconscious will react to revelatory moments. When you have a "eureka!" insight about yourself, you reprogram the beastie, and it can have an immediate effect.

Revelations can't be manufactured. However, doing artwork, reading books, and viewing other artists' work can help you gain more insights. Don't just scroll Instagram. Go to the museum, art galleries, or library and look at large picture books.

*There is also another way
to speed up reprogramming the mind.*

If you work at it, you can create a reframing of the way you see things. A reframe of a problem can change your thinking fairly quickly. This is called mindset, and it's a known phenomenon in psychology. Mindset is embodied in the placebo effect.

Just believing that a pill will help you get better makes many people… get better. It is such a strong part of the human equation that whenever they do trials for new medications, they have to include a placebo control group to compare the results of each group.

Otherwise, all the improvements might just be from the mindset of getting the medication and not the actual effect of the medication. (Here's a great, quick, and fun resource for this: the hidden brain podcast Reframing Your Reality, Parts 1 and 2, July 18 and 25, 2022)

Sometimes, we think something is negative when it is the opposite. That means we need to reframe it. I told you about one of these reframes just recently. That is, artists tend to believe that looking at their work and not liking it proves they're not artists. That's the wrong frame.

This ability to evaluate your own work is an essential skill all artists need. Now, you can start believing this correct viewpoint. Only by clearly seeing how your work needs to improve can you ever improve it.

Another backward framing happens when you don't see much progress daily. The reality is that artists improve in bursts after a period of struggle. Hang in there. You'll soon get to that next exciting growth point.

Now we've reframed another negative idea and turned it into a positive expectation. If you internalize and dwell on these positive reframings, your subconscious beast will follow.

The first and second sections of this book are devoted to discussing misconceptions. All we've been doing is ReFRAMING. You can continue to reframe any negative ideas that persist any time you want. It just takes identifying a negative idea and figuring out how to look at it from a different, more positive perspective.

If you review the earlier chapters every month for a year, you will change your thinking about being an artist and embed that change into your subconscious.

You now have three powerful new
tools to start changing
your mindset—

1. *Tell yourself positive things.*
Be kind and encouraging.

2. *Reframe the negative ideas.*

3. *Practice, study, and view art*
to have more eureka insights.

Starting right now, tell yourself every day that you are on the way to becoming the artist you want to be. Make notes for yourself. Hide them everywhere so you continually find them unexpectedly. If that's not your style, invent something that is, and that is self-encouraging.

Every time you make work you aren't happy with, tell yourself it's a good thing, that it's the correct and natural process, and that you're on the same path as all artists. You are making Learners, which means you're learning a ton of new stuff. Tell yourself to have patience and to practice so you can keep improving. You will.

You were born an artist,
and you know it.

PART TWO (2)

Building Up

I AM AN
ARTIST

Chapter 9
The Blueprint

To build your new sense of self as an artist, you need a blueprint, a comprehensive guide for the systems of art, what components each system uses, and how they fit together.

Art Systems

The most basic operations that art can be divided into were surprisingly difficult to figure out. I remember learning sets of elements and principles in art school. These aren't things I think of as systems, but neither were any other lists of things or steps I've created over the years, which seemed to be the simple model I was looking for. Nothing seemed to fit into how artists live their lives creating art.

I finally started writing down everything I do while being a visual artist. After a while, I studied these notes and could see some connections. After a few attempts at simplifying them into a small number of basic categories, I finally arrived at four primary systems I call THE FOUR COMPONENTS OF VISUAL ART.

- Input
- Supplies
- Make
- Goals

These can be arranged into two categories of RAW MATERIALS & PRODUCTION:

RAW MATERIALS	PRODUCTION
Input	Make
Supplies	Goals

They can also be arranged by two categories: CRE-
ATIVE & PRACTICAL.

CREATIVE	PRACTICAL
Input	Goals
Make	Supplies

They can also be arranged into two final groups: IN-
TELLECTUAL ("IN THE MIND") & PHYSICAL.

INTELLECTUAL	PHYSICAL
Input	Supplies
Goals	Make

It's important to understand all three ways to ar-
range the four components because it helps us realize what we are doing and how to manage ourselves.
Some artists don't enjoy dealing with the practical
aspects as opposed to the creative, and some don't
enjoy intellectual exercises as much as physical exercises. Ignore one of them for long, and it will negatively affect everything you do.

It is essential, though, for every artist to be at least somewhat proficient in each of these four areas. Each one supports the others, so they are all inextricably linked. Ignore one of them enough, which will negatively affect everything you do. For instance, having bad brushes can make you think you're not a good painter because some brushes will completely sabotage your ability to paint well.

It's similar to the electricity being off, which will prevent the water heater from working, which means you don't have a hot shower and won't be able to operate the heating and air system. Everything is connected in your house of art.

It's probably too early to know right now, which things will bring you the most excitement or what areas will provide you the most challenges. Knowing this is power! You can find ways to balance things once you understand your weakest links. I have learned several methods that help me, and I'll share them with you in the second book.

If you shy away from non-creative things, then apply your creativity to make those things more attractive to work on.

A great way to remember these four components is to say this self-encouraging phrase: "Input and supplies make my goals."

Write this down and say it to yourself often. You'll start to believe it, and more importantly, so will your subconscious.

Knowing the systems that need to be used is essential to knowing how to operate. With a home, you know there is electricity, plumbing, gas, internet, heating, cooling, and more. You also know how to run those things because tools exist to help you use them, like light switches, knobs, thermostats, and faucets.

Likewise, you know how to use a pencil, eraser, pen, and brush, and probably how to mix some important colors, like orange from yellow and red.

When you turn up the knob on the thermostat, if the house stays cold and you don't know how to fix it, you call the HVAC company.

When you draw something, if it doesn't look the way you want, and you don't know how to fix it … there is actually no one to call.

You need DIY art.

Good news! It's way easier and much more fun to learn DIY art than it is to learn how to fix your HVAC system. Believe me, because I've done both.

Remember the drawing of the glass? That is exactly what I'm talking about. Learning how to make a fundamental 3D shape such as a cylinder look more accurate is fun and rewarding. Then you know how to do it forever.

You might forget at some point and draw the old way; but it's a cinch to see what needs to be changed (remember that seeing what your art needs is a skill you already have) and correct it. It's much, much easier than getting into an attic and rewiring a heating system.

Making stripes on a rounded object look realistic is similar to making the bottom of a cylinder look realistic. Remember the stripes on the back of the animal? The application is different, but many of the principles are the same. The bark on a tree sometimes has rounded lines, too. This cylinder example is found all over the place.

If you can master how to draw the 3D-shape (form) cylinder, cube, and sphere, you can apply those three most fundamental 3D shapes (forms), to most of what you'll ever need to draw.

There is no magic wand I can give you to speed up your artistic development, but once you start building, it's a fantastic thing. You're going to be working on your very own talent. I guarantee it will be full of fun and rewards. If you don't give up, you'll have a great source of enjoyment and entertainment.

THE FOUR COMPONENTS OF VISUAL ART (EXPANDED)

Each of THE FOUR COMPONENTS has two or three sections.

INPUT has Intellectual and Creative Raw Materials:

- Inspiration
- Dreaming
- Development

SUPPLIES has Physical and Practical Raw Materials:

- Media
- Tools
- Space

MAKE has Physical and Creative Production:

- Learners
- Keepers
- Evaluation
- Experimentation

GOALS has Intellectual and Practical Production:

- Vision
- Purpose

Let's define these sections in more detail.

Input

Inspiration

Artists get their inspiration from experiencing things outside themselves that affect them somehow. This can be from nature, human discourse and interactions, and works by other artists, visual or otherwise, such as music and poetry.

Dreaming

The artist thinks about what they want to do. Having big ideas similarly moves us to inspiration, but it comes from within.

Development

Artists must improve and grow. Even artists who have found a niche always practice staying in shape and creating experimental work to discover new ways of doing things. New artists will be developing most of the time, taking courses, learning from instructors, websites, and books, and practicing a lot. A new artist will create mostly Learners, while an experienced artist will create mostly Keepers. All artists create both kinds of work to some degree.

MAKING

Learners

When you make something you like or don't like, it's always a Learner's work and is, therefore, highly valuable to your development as an artist.

Keepers

Artists make work they like. The goal for all artists is to create works that they are satisfied with and that have value beyond their own learning experiences. These works fulfill their vision and are used to reach their goals.

Evaluation

Artists must constantly stop and look at what they're doing to decide if they are doing things the way they want to. "Is this part accurate or not?" Did I maintain my overall emphasis when I added this color?"

Experimentation

Artists get better when they stretch. Getting outside the box, or the lines that create those boxes, is essential. Development requires trying new techniques and new materials. How do you know what you can do until you try?

GOALS

Vision

Artists need a personal vision that guides them. Your own expression is what makes your work unique. Copying other styles can help you learn, but experimentation and practice should lead you to something that isn't quite like the other artists' work that you liked at first. Artists will make something a little bit new, something that you are doing in your own way.

Purpose

Artists can't help but communicate with their work. Your purposes are what that message is and what the work does for others and the artists themselves. This can be as simple as making money or making people relax. It can be about social justice and change. It can try to be all of those things together. Some artists do separate sets of work for different purposes.

SUPPLIES

Media

Artists can use any media available to them. Some use a wide variety, seeking or striving for new looks from new media combinations, while others stick to just a few things they know well.

Tools

Artists need to understand how to choose and care for their physical materials, making their work as easy and enjoyable as possible.

Space

Artists need to work in a studio, which can be a temporary setup or a special room dedicated to this purpose.

THE COMPLETE BLUEPRINT
OF ALL ELEMENTS

The next part is an outline. It's only a blueprint. It is not a guide for how to build or fix the things in the blueprint. How-to guides for each component will be in Part Three.

The following is not a list but an index. It's a tool for discovery.

Do

Use this as a resource to organize your thoughts so that you are not overwhelmed. Use it to drill down to a specific item that you may enjoy working on.

You can come here any time to look through the outline and find out where things fit. It should encourage you to think about the things you want and how to make them happen.

- Take one thing at a time.
- It's fine to leave most things to another day.
- OK, it's essential to leave most things to another day.

Don't

Skim the outline! Don't think of it as a list. Taking it as a whole, or thinking briefly about more than one item at a time can make you feel overwhelmed, which can paralyze your progress instead of leading you to action.

In other words, do not look at this and generalize, making this into some kind of mile-long to-do list. This outline is the opposite, as it helps you drill down to specifics, so you can focus and work on one thing, instead of getting lost in giant concepts.

In the *Artist's Missing Manual,* there is one chapter devoted to organizing your thoughts and managing them in a way that keeps you focused on simple goals, ONE AT A TIME.

SYSTEM ONE
Personal Development

LEARNING

Learning: Sources

- Books
- Classes and tutorials
- In person
- Online (live or recorded)
- Apps and websites

Learning: Subjects

- Accuracy
- Three Steps
- Forms (cube, sphere, cylinder)
- Light and shadow
- Media techniques
- Content
- People

- Landscape
- Still life
- Animals
- Abstract
- Imagination
- Color mixing
- Color theory
- Composition
- Preparation
- Preservation
- Presentation
- Transactions & business
- Experimenting (also found in the system)
- Making
- Thinking (writing and journaling about your work)

- Inspiration
- Nature
- Photography
- Artworks by others
- Online
- Museums and Galleries
- Experiences
- Travel
- Stories & News
- Relationships

SYSTEM TWO
Your Vision

Style—Working toward your own distinct look
Messages—Everything conveys an idea
Media—The materials you decide to use
Technique—How you execute your work, with movement and surface interactions

System Three
Making the Stuff

- Preparation
- Reference
- Photos
- On-site
- Life Set-up
- Setting Up Materials
- Experimenting (playing and stretching your experience and ideas)
- Practicing (learning the current subject matter)
- Drawing
- Quick sketches
- Detailed studies

- Thumbnails for Composition
- Color Roughs
- Do-overs/Learners
- Expressing: The Art!
- Surface treatment (underpainting, adding texture, etc.)
- Drawing Guidelines
- Using the Three Steps to Accuracy
- Frame Proportions
- Big Shapes
- Details
- Main Event (The best and biggest part!)
- Finishing/Evaluating

SYSTEM FOUR
The Stuff You Need to Make Stuff

MEDIA

DRAWING
Pencil
Charcoal
Ink
Conte Crayon

There is always more…

PAINTING
Oil
Acrylic
Watercolor

More…

PRINTMAKING
Etching
Wood/Lino cut
Monoprints
Collage
Pastels
Encaustic
More…
Sculpture
Wood
Metal
Stone

More…

Tools
Containers
Carrying devices
Lighting
Brushes
Pencils
Pastels
Cutters
More…
Surfaces
Panels
Canvas
Paper

More…

SYSTEM FIVE
Purpose

What you are going to do with your art—

- Audience
- Presentation (framing, mounting, installing)
- Effects (make change)
- Transactions (trade)
- Protection (copyrights)

ART
DRAW
WATER COLORS
INK
PASTEL
PAINT

Chapter 10

Joy of the Journey

Artists are explorers. Once you begin exploring, you're in the game! You never graduate or arrive at some kind of level that makes you suddenly a "real" artist. Goals are just for moving in the direction you want to explore next.

Often I have parents come into the studio to ask how we motivate students. When this happens, I've learned that they're looking for the wrong answers:

- We'll push them harder!
- We'll reach some goals!
- We'll make them successful!"

Parents sometimes believe that having a coach, pushing for progress and even yelling at the student, is the best way to make them a better skater, ball player, or gymnast. Relentless practice and dedication are glorified in our culture because they often create amazing athletes. Or piano players. Or mathematicians. Or whatever you have heard about.

Art is not the same. Art is composing, not playing. Creativity comes from a place within and seeks self-expression. You cannot push this forward from the outside. You can't make a person want to fulfill their creative desires.

The one thing that motivates an artist the most, is removing whatever causes frustration when creating artwork.

I once had a student who came to my classes and was amazingly adept at drawing technique and accuracy. She had studied in Asia for many years and was going to go to college in another year.

I had never had a student who was so stressed about their art. She limited herself to use a few precise methods of pencil work and complained that she could never do it to her satisfaction. Everything frustrated her.

All I could do was encourage her and try to show her more expressive and enjoyable methods—but it didn't help. She was convinced that severe discipline was the only way to achieve the correct art goals and to move forward. She hated art class. She hated her work. She was so unhappy. She quit soon afterward.

I wish I could have convinced her that the harsh methods she was pursuing were not related to her creativity. Technique is only important if it helps you reach your personal creative goals. She seemed to be trying to reach other people's goals, and it was not joyful for her.

I hear mistaken expectations being applied by artists, onto themselves, all the time:

- "I'm too slow."
- "I'm too fast."
- "I'm too rigid."
- "I'm too sloppy."
- "I'm too loose."
- "I'm too tight."

I could fill pages with these statements. None of them are accurate.

All artists have their own pace, their own tendencies, and their own styles. Artists need to let go of trying to do things the "right" way and start discovering how to do things the way that is best for their work and their own vision.

Let's reframe the previous negative statements:

- "I like to work methodically."
- "I'm a bit impatient doing my work, which creates a lot of energy in it!"
- "I love order and my work shows a lot of structure."
- "My crazy studio leads me to be more creative."
- "My style is very expressive."
- "Realism is what I'm doing now."

This doesn't mean that everything an artist creates is great. That kind of thinking is a trap. It also doesn't mean that the most obvious solution to bring your ideas and art work together will be what you actually need.

For example, let's pretend a beginning artist has a vague and loose technique, with soft edges and low contrast, but they want to create very clear, specific ideas. They like things that are tightly rendered or even photo-realistic. They choose complicated subjects with lots of objects and interactions.

Their work looks awkward and is difficult to understand because the loose and airy style they like and the complicated and busy content they like are not working well together. Their artwork is not as appreciated as they want it to be.

One way our fictional artist might address this is to dismiss critique entirely, deciding that the artist is above the need to conform to others expectations. This is easy, requiring no additional work or investment from the artist. The entire responsibility for evaluating the art is moved to the viewer.

The artist begins to believe they only create good work, even when people reject it. So nothing changes, and the artist is still under-appreciated.

Another direction the artist could take is to abandon their style. They can work against their tendencies to paint soft and loose. They may work for years to create a tight and controlled style that is different from what they like to do. They eventually realize that they don't enjoy creating this work. They might end up abandoning art as a result.

Yet another direction is for the artist to abandon the content they want to convey, and try to paint something that looks soft, like landscapes. They find that it doesn't motivate them, even though people like their work more. Inspiration is lost and again they don't enjoy creating their art.

None of these "solutions" address the real problem of adjusting in a way that resolves all the issues at play. They're just easy.

This artist needs to experiment and explore. Then they can discover new ways to change their work yet not abandon their tendencies, likes, style, or preferred content. This is hard! It takes some work. The example I gave is a difficult one, and almost anyone would choose one of the three directions, which could eventually lead to unfulfillment.

Most people don't realize complex solutions can be found by experimenting, but this is vital to artists' development. Exploration is a huge part of what being an artist is all about. Having a difficult problem in reconciling your style, your vision, or your purpose is one way that could lead to new ideas and projects.

The artist who takes the time and experiments often may find many different solutions to their issues. In our example, adding bold outlines might solve the whole thing perfectly. Adding color and contrast to define areas may also be another way to go. The point is, no one knows until you try.

Art is not automatic. Artists are not these amazing superheroes who know exactly the right way to create their work. They have to struggle and try different approaches—all the time.

Some people believe that artists only create viable artwork. This is a misconception, especially early in the artist's journey. Taking new paths is the only way to find new and exciting places. You have to be willing to hit the inevitable dead ends along with the discoveries.

It's a huge process that is always changing and is always a bit of a challenge. That means if you feel challenged, you are a normal artist. That's how it works.

Risks are good, but you want a balance between experimentation and what you like. You don't want to go against your own vision and personal style tendencies. You want to make them work for you. If you push yourself to go to places that are not fun or natural, it's likely to take the joy of creating away. That is the last thing you want to do.

So you need goals, but you don't need a bunch of rules to make those goals somehow more reachable. The goals are there to point you in the right direction, for now. The goals should never be in charge.

That's why, in my classes, we have Three Rules.

Three Rules

1. The first rule is… NOT TOO MANY RULES. Artists are supposed to think outside the box, you know.

2. The second rule is BE NICE, which has three ap-plications:

- Be nice to others of course.
- Be nice to your tools, and your materials.
- Be nice to yourself—this is the hard one.

3. The third rule is… NO MISTAKES ALLOWED!

I enjoy getting students' attention with this one. Everyone has been listening and enjoying my talk about not having too many rules and being nice. And then I say something super-rule-oriented and not very nice at all. Heads snap up in shock.

This scary statement touches a very fearful place for artists, that of making a mistake. That's exactly why I've suddenly thrown this unexpected firecracker out there. It exposes the fear, and that allows me to pop that bubble of insecurity into oblivion with my explanation, below.

You cannot make a mistake as an artist. It's impossible. You can only learn new things, even when you make something you hate. Everything—every single thing you do—will add to your knowledge and your experience as an artist. It's all good, even when it's bad. Yes, I said this earlier, but you need to hear it often. You need to be released from fear and expectations.

*The world needs happy artists.
Don't push yourself too hard.
Don't try to live up to false expectations.
Expression and fulfillment come
from within you, from your heart.*

CHAPTER 11
New Chapter: The Lifeline

Here is how to pull yourself out of the quicksand of discouragement...

In football, it's against the rules to pile onto the quarterback after he's been tackled. That's because it's human nature for everyone to jump all over him.

People do this a lot. We pile onto anyone who is down, amplifying the negatives when we see them. We especially like to find things to complain about.

We've talked about being nice to ourselves, but we need a little more direction on how to do it.

All artists get discouraged with their work. When your art is not looking the way you want, the frustrating problem you're experiencing can grow until it starts to swallow you up. It's like quicksand. Especially if we generalize meaning or if we mistakenly apply the frustration about one problem to our entire work.

You need to resist piling on. Try not to increase the self-criticism. Your tendency to amplify the fact that you have a problem is so strong that it is hard to even notice that you are piling on, but you need to counteract the urge to sink into a pit of despair.

You can't counteract sinking by struggling though. That would look like furiously reworking the art in multiple ways but without a plan, eventually destroying much of it, or it might be by abandoning the work or throwing the thing in the trash. Resistance is futile if you stay in a generalization mode. Again, problems are specific.

Problems—They're Always Specific

You need to fix that problem, but you can't do it while you're in the pit. You must first find a rope to pull yourself out, or all that blind struggling will just suck you deeper down.

A metaphorical rope represents something very specific in the real world, which is simply looking for, and finding, one good part of the artwork in front of you.

Find One Good Thing

This is a core element of the instructor training at my art school. Whenever someone is discouraged about their work, we have to find something good. It's always there. When a teacher walks up to view a frustrated student's work, it's always easy to find the good things, because we are not stuck in the quicksand. We can see more clearly.

Often, the student does not want us to do this, which is so surprising. They are having a moment of despair, and, like playing with a loose tooth even when it hurts, they want to dwell in that despair. The young artists are sitting there, piling onto themselves, looking for more and more bad things.

It's hard to notice this happening in a big classroom. After teaching a lesson, the room will be full of different activities: a bunch of kids are laughing at their own jokes, a student is making noise, disrupting the class on purpose; another group is arguing about some TV show I like and want to defend; several people are happily painting; one student is very quiet, slowly moving their brush around; and another student has stopped working and pulled out their phone.

The last two are the ones who need immediate help. One is showing discouraged body language. The other is escaping.

If I walk up and ask a generalized question like, "Are you okay with your work?" or "Do you like what you're doing?" they will say, "Sure." While there are students who are honest and tell us they're unhappy about something, usually we have to draw it out. We have to ask specific questions instead of generalizations.

"What's your favorite thing about this work?" "Which area are you struggling with the most right now?" These are specific questions that you have to answer with more specific answers.

However, the first thing we do is walk up and Find One Good Thing. We start with a compliment. Then we ask some specific questions. It's so easy! This two-part method works like magic, creating meaningful dialog and breaking the escalation of the negative self-criticism.

You can train yourself to "find one good thing" yourself. Find something positive that will work like a rope, a lifeline, to pull you out—instead of sinking into the negative. Once you do this, you'll probably see a lot more good things.

This only works for students when I am truthful. A simple generalization, such as, "I think this painting is fantastic" is most likely a lie. You can clearly see if it's not. If I say something like that, I immediately lose the student's trust. I have to get specific about it and find a good thing I truly believe is good. So you must look for real good things. You can.

"This color right here is amazing," "I like how accurate this part is," "I nailed the expression on that face," or "The balance in this composition is great. It's making everything work overall well together."

Good things are easy to find because no artist creates a work where every single thing is bad. Most
work is typically pretty good. You can get into a funk
because one bad part has simply become so frustrating that it eclipses the rest.

Once you get free of the pit, then it's time to drill
down to the specific problem so you can fix it. You
can remove the frustration so your art keeps improving.

BEGIN!
ONE
TWO
THREE
FEUR

Chapter 12
Making a Personal Plan

Having a plan does two very important things for you. First, it helps you do the things that you need to do the most and avoid the things that get in your way.

Secondly, it frees you up to focus on one thing at a time, which may be the next step in a series of steps, or sometimes just the thing that you're excited about today.

You don't have to play by any rules, because you are in charge. But not having to play by rules can be aimless and frustrating if you don't follow some kind of plan. Have a plan, but check your plan to make sure it will make you happy and not overwhelm you.

There are two kinds of plans:

- The long-term plan
- The short-term plan

Your *long-term plan* falls under GOALS, in the Vision and Purpose sections, while the *short-term plan* is day-to-day and practical.

Your short-term plan is about making time and space and managing all your other sections. This is under SUPPLIES, in the time section. You can't make art without a decent supply of time.

The Long Term

The long-term plan is about your goals and your vision. Most working artists generate a vision statement. That statement also includes the goals the artist hopes to achieve with this vision.

A long-term plan may only be directed towards your goals for a year or two, and may change during that time. It is simply the next station on your journey as an artist as you see it.

Your vision is what you want your art to look like, conveying the ideas you want to communicate, what you want people to get out of it. It may include your media and technique of choice.

Your purpose is what you want to do with your art. *Is it primarily for you, or for others?* You may want it to be equal in that respect. *What do you want from your art? What do you want others to get from your art?*

- Joyful emotions?
- Healing of painful emotions?
- Experience?
- Peace?
- Sharing?
- Teaching?
- Income?
- Useful objects with beauty?
- Other?

Artists have traditionally been told that there is only one legitimate goal: Be professionally successful.

The implication is clear (if completely false): If you don't see successful income-producing-art fame as your goal, you should not even try to become an artist. The dark side of this is that if others don't see that kind of success as a possibility, then they tell you to stop trying.

While other endeavors have a degree of pressure to perform and succeed, they also encourage casual versions of that performance. Only visual art completely disdains the casual practitioner. This elitist outlook eclipses any view other than the masterful genius who can rise to fame. Artists are viewed as priests and priestesses who are adorned by their own inner muse whom no one else can ever understand. All others are lay people.

Home artists—the casual practitioners—are ridiculed, excluded, and discouraged. Think about it. What other endeavor experiences this kind of exclusion? Every other activity is the opposite, encouraging anyone who is doing it simply for the fun and joy it brings.

People may laugh when I dance, because I'm not much of a dancer; but they don't scowl at me. I can't play tennis very well, but my friends ask me to play with them, anyway.

When we see artwork that is not on a professional level, we often grimace at it. We even get embarrassed for the artist. We shake our heads and wonder who told them they could do this.

Are they doing it simply for the fun and joy it brings them? Why do we feel like it's our job to rob them of this experience? It makes us so much more afraid to try it ourselves.

What if your goal is to give your art as gifts, or make personal cards to send to friends and family? What if you just want to hang it on your own walls? Your goals are entirely up to you, and there is no reason to feel like you have to have your art hang in a gallery or a museum someday.

You can decide to do whatever you want with the art you make. You can even paint over it, if that makes you happy; and just decide to make more. You can set up a booth on the street and give your art away to everyone who passes by.

*Money is not the only way
to show art appreciation.
Art does not have to be your career.*

Often, a career in art makes it harder to be creative for yourself. At the end of a day working in commercial art, I was beat, and my creative juices were all used up. I rarely painted, even though I wanted to.

*All you need to do is
what will make you happy.*

However, if selling your work actually is what will make you happy, then that is your legitimate and attainable goal. It does not mean you have to rise to the top. Just keep after it, developing your talent in your own way and at your own pace. Find the people who like your work, and figure out a way to sell it to them at a price that makes everyone happy. It's all up to you.

Energy comes and goes.

One very good way to tell if you are on the right track for your art's purpose is to determine the direction of the energy flow when you're MAKING art.

If you get more energized when you're making artwork, then you're doing it the way you need to. This is energy-producing.

If you feel like making art is hard or begins to drain you at the moment you begin, then it is energy-reducing. That means something is not the way you need it to be. You can't sustain that.

Making art should be fun. It might be relaxing or make you move more. I tend to dance around when I'm working. The thing is that you should be energized in some way. You should get a lot of joy out of being in the studio and making things.

241

You may be tired at the end of your session; but, it's satisfying, and you won't want to stop. This is why you create.

This is important—

> *If you don't have energy-producing time when creating your artwork, you need to find out why. What are the things that take the energy away? It is likely an idea you have from others, not from yourself.*

If you're trying to please a mentor, a family member, or even an imaginary group of viewers of your work, you are working for someone else. That will suck the energy right out of you.

Go back to your dreams. Find out what makes you the most excited and apply that to your vision and your purpose. You can do it. You have everything you need right there inside of you.

The Short Term

This is your day-to-day plan.

A lot of artists find this part to be difficult, but it's also essential. Without a plan to make your art today, it's like trying to find your way through the jungle in the dark. Everything is all around you, but you can't get anywhere.

Why do we get overwhelmed? What makes our heads spin around in circles when we have a few things to do? Why can't we focus?

Artists are creative, and we have lots of things we want to do. All of these things are floating around us, and when we think of one, we see all the others, and we become distracted. We can't figure out how to start.

Your brain can only handle two things at once—the thing you're doing now and the thing you're going to do next. I can prove this.

Imagine a gray room with no doors or windows. Now, add a yellow ball and move it around the room, bouncing gently off the walls. You can imagine it going fast or slowly.

Now add a red ball. Even though this is double the mental work, you can do it. You can manage two balls easily because you always manage two hands.

But now add a blue ball. Yeah, this is why it's so hard to juggle. You can manage the first two balls as a group or quickly jump between two and one and back again. Then, the blue ball can be managed to a degree, but you can't keep track of all three balls simultaneously unless you make one of them do a simple pattern. Your brain is only designed to completely control two things.

If you have three things to do today, you have *too many* to hold in your head. You can't do two things at one time. You can only do one thing and start imagining how you'll do the next thing. That's your capacity as a human being.

I can't tell you how often I've been completely overwhelmed by the "things I must do right away," almost in a panic. But then I made a list, only to find that there were only three things I had to do, sometimes four or five.

Once I make a list—poof!
The overwhelmed feeling just disappears.

Why does this work? The things I have to do are the same. Well, it turns out that our brain cannot tell the difference between three things and thirty. Each number is simply more than we can manage in our mind, so they become a cloud of unknown tasks swimming around us, totally out of our control.

When you write them down, you can see right away that one of them is the first thing to do. A list is the best tool you can ever employ.

I have a standard list of steps for creating artwork that ensures I don't skip something essential, which keeps me on track. It's the Seven Steps For Making Art. This list and more methods for list management are in my second book, *The Artist's Missing Manual—A Comprehensive Guide for How to Manage Yourself As an Artist.*

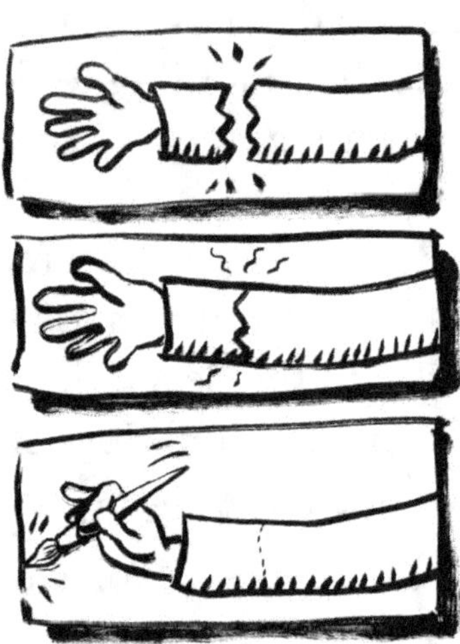

Chapter 13
Healing Feels Good

I hesitated to write a chapter about healing because this is a book about being an artist. Being an artist usually has some pretty rough history associated with it though.

Almost every adult artist I talk to has been hurt by someone—specifically about being an artist. That means there are deep wounds in many of us. It calls for a chapter on healing, even if it's a short one, which it will be.

One thing I have learned is that everyone needs help. I would not have amounted to much without the support I received from others at critical times in my life.

Most artists, including myself, are super individualists, though. Getting any kind of assistance will damage our hotshot persona, a persona that we hold quite dear.

But the other thing I have learned is that leaning on others is a form of strength. It's a quiet admission that none of us is superwoman or superman and that mental health is as essential as physical health.

Emotional pain doesn't fade. You just get used to it, sort of. Pain that is associated with your very identity is huge. You can't "just move on." You need to find peace. It is essential.

Finding the right way to heal may take trial and error. Finding your way with your art will take patience and determination, and so, too, will finding your path to healing.

If you become discouraged with what a person says or something a book states, then move to another source. Find what works for you. Don't generalize and give into the idea that you can't do this or that it's not worth it. Your health is definitely worth it.

*There are several kinds of
mental and emotional healing
that we need to pursue.*

One is about training the Inner Beastie, and we've covered that. Another is also within ourselves, but is uncontrollable, because it's like having a physical flaw we were born with. I don't feel bad about being nearsighted, because I didn't cause it to happen.

The last thing is when someone has said something or done something to you. This is externally-influenced emotional health.

Catching a cold overwhelms our immune system, but only for a week or so. Then our defenses kick in and our body can heal itself. Amazingly, we do not have an auto-immune mental health system. On top of that, there is the irony that we believe mental health is easier to deal with than physical health.

We know humans all have physical illnesses, and we understand that these need our attention. Some are chronic, like an allergy that causes us to conform to a special diet or take a medicine. Some are very temporary, such as a cold or food poisoning.

But we ignore and avoid our emotional trauma, and we even believe we can think our way out of mental illnesses, such as anxiety or depression.

Emotional and mental damage is just like physical damage, in two ways. You are debilitated, and you can't make yourself well by pretending you're okay. A sprained ankle will take a long time to heal and will always be weak if you just keep walking on it. An open wound can get much worse if not tended to. You can't run with a limp, and you can't fix a broken leg with your mind.

We tend to be overly optimistic sometimes with ourselves. We think, "That wasn't abuse, that was just a little bit mean. I'm okay. I'm tougher than that."

It doesn't matter how severe your wound is.
Even a paper cut can still hurt badly.
It still needs to heal.

Mental Health Issues

We treat mental health differently than physical health, because we believe the mind can fix the mind.

Well, it can't. You can't simply think your way out of pain, anxiety, depression, or ADHD, etc. You need help from people with skills, tools, medicines, and training.

When I was young, I took a personality test that, according to the testing person, said I was the most chill person on the entire planet. This was strange to learn, because I had struggled with anxiety.

When I first began to have panic attacks, I called it, "The Nameless Dread." It would come out of nowhere, but it felt like I had been told I was going to die. I saw visions I won't describe.

I was up all night, heart racing, trying desperately to latch onto something that was causing my panic. I would always wonder if I was sick and my body knew it. Any little pain or ache meant I was dying. It was ridiculous, yet, to me, it was the most serious thing.

Finally, I told my doctor. He had a friend who had gone through the same thing, so he realized immediately what was going on. Just knowing helped some, but I had to get help in the form of medication. I eventually discovered that diet made a huge difference, too.

Most of the people I know with mental health issues—and that is quite a lot more people than I ever imagined—have needed to work on it, and continually depend on a plan and/or medications. It's just like any other illness. You have to take care of yourself.

Emotional Trauma

When someone hurts us, we have emotional damage. We also, surprisingly, have a physical reaction to that damage, which can continue to affect us for years, sometimes the rest of our lives. One response to conflict is the fight or flight response. When we've had trauma, that fight or flight response doesn't go away. It comes back over and over, making us react in ways that we don't want to and usually don't understand.

But it doesn't have to be that way.

One of the biggest and best tools for emotional healing is also the one we tend to avoid the most: forgiveness. Forgiveness is hard, because it means we have to quit enjoying the vilification of the very person who made us hurt. We get a lot of reward from that vilification. We love to complain, and we need to blame.

But I'm here to tell you something truly profound. Forgiveness is amazingly wonderful once you let go of your bitterness. Forgiveness has nothing to do with the person who wronged you. It is for you. It is like being released from a cage.

In mid-life, I realized that my entire journey in improving my life to that point was all about realizing I was hurt and angry, and needed to forgive people. When I had this revelation, I tasked myself with finding everyone who had done something mean or hurtful to me or to people I loved.

One by one, I found places in me that were distorted by these damaging moments. Some of these people were dead, and some I didn't even know their names.

But it was surprisingly easy sometimes to just let go and forgive them. To try and understand that they were also victims, but that they had not been able to forgive their abusers.

Sometimes forgiving a particular person is more difficult than forgiving others. Pain can be complex, but forgiveness can be possible. We can always forgive, even when the hurt is incomprehensible. I can't tell you how to do it, but you can find a way if you want to.

Forgiveness is the path to true healing and freedom. I encourage you to consider forgiveness. It takes deliberate and, sometimes, ongoing effort. But it gets better and better! This isn't always something you can do on your own.

We need to be open to finding what works, which may mean working with a counselor or others who are professionally qualified.

Healing must be part of your plan.

Be kind to yourself. Treat your pain like you would treat a dear friend's pain. Find help. Find the people you need to forgive. Keep after it, and find a path to freedom.

SEEK HEALING

Thank you for reading. Now you understand that whoever told you not to pursue art, or that you weren't a true artist, was absolutely 100% WRONG.

You've discovered that not only were they acting out of self-doubt, but that the whole of society is set up to misinform artists about who they are. You learned that even the art world experts disagree about what makes art good or can agree on how to talk about it. You understand how confusion clouds everything about the values of art.

All of these mythical ideas that were holding back can now move to the background, so you can get on with developing your art. Now it's time to start! Make your lists and plans, and give yourself a lot of breaks.

You have the blueprint
to make your foundation
and build your dreams.

*Start now, if you haven't already.
You can do it! You are an artist,
after all, and artists can
change the world.*

Dennas Davis | *Artist*

About the Author

Dennas Davis is an illustrator, painter, teacher, and founder of Firstlight Art Academy, Dennas has been a professional artist for over forty years. He is the original illustrator of *The Beginner's Bible,* and has worked for Disney, Forbes, Nabisco, RCA records, CBS, Sony, and Betty Crocker. Dennas has over five million books in print worldwide in over thirty languages.

To Contact Dennas Davis
dennasd.com
@dennas

Sign up for

ARTIBLES

where Dennas regularly posts new insights
and techniques for artists. It's free. Just go to

www.dennasdavis.substack.com

COMING SOON

The Artist's Missing Manual—
A Comprehensive Guide for
How to Manage Yourself As an Artist

www.ingramcontent.com/pod-product-compliance
Lightning Source LLC
Chambersburg PA
CBHW081337160726
48000CB00010B/3136